Return on or before the
last date stamped below.

Kingston College
Kingston Hall Road
Kingston upon Thames
KT1 2AQ

Serbia Through the Ages

Alex N. Dragnich

EAST EUROPEAN MONOGRAPHS, BOULDER, CO
DISTRIBUTED BY COLUMBIA UNIVERSITY PRESS, NY
2004

EAST EUROPEAN MONOGRAPHS, NO. DCXLIII

Copyright 2004 by Alex N. Dragnich

ISBN: 0-88033-541-6

Library of Congress Control Number: 2004108566

Printed in the United States of America

Contents

The Growth of Serbia, 1817–1913

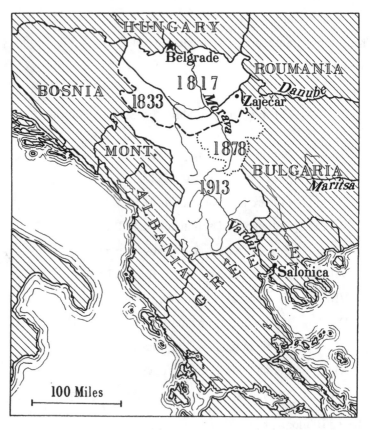

Map by Charlotte Carlson

A Note on Pronunciation

The Serbo-Croatian language is phonetic, but because there are some letters that do no appear in English it is necessary to use diacritical marks over letters or to combine two letters to produce the desired sound. Also, certain letters that have differing sounds in English will have only one sound in Serbo-Croatian. It is hoped that the following will be helpful.

a	—	a as in father
c	—	ts as in mats
ć	—	ch as in rich
č	—	ch as in chalk
dj	—	g as in George
e	—	e as in pet
i	—	i as in machine
j	—	y as in yet
lj	—	li as in million
nj	—	ni as in dominion
o	—	o as in over
š	—	sh as in shawl
u	—	u as in rule
ž	—	j as in French *jour*

Chronology of Serbian and Montenegrin Rulers

SERBIA

1168–1196	Nemanja, founder of the Nemanjić dynasty
1196–1223	Stefan Prvovenčani (First Crowned), second son of Nemanja
1223–1233	Radoslav, first son of Stefan
1233–1242	Vladislav, second son of Stefan
1242–1276	Uroš I, third son of Stefan
1276–1281	Dragutin, elder son of Uroš I
1281–1321	Milutin, younger son of Dragutin
1321–1331	Stefan Dečanski (Uroš III), son of Milutin
1331–1355	Dušan (Stefan Uroš IV), son of Stefan Dečanski
1355–1371	Uroš V, son of Dušan
1372–1389	Prince Lazar (Hrebeljanović)
1389–1427	Despot Stefan (Lazarević), son of Lazar
1427–1456	Djurdje Branković, nephew of Despot Stefan
1456–1458	Lazar, son of Djurdje
1459–1804	Serbia under Turkish rule
1804–1813	Karadjordje, founder of Karadjordjević dynasty
1815–1839	Miloš Obrenović, founder of Obrenović dynasty
1839–1858	Alexander Karadjordjević, son of Karadjordje
1859–1860	Miloš Obrenović
1860–1868	Mihailo Obrenović
1868–1889	Milan Obrenović
1889–1903	Alexander Obrenović
1903–1921	Peter I Karadjordjević
1921–1934	Alexander I Karadjordjević
1934–1941	Regency for Peter II Karadjordjević, son of Alexander

MONTENEGRO
(center of Serbdom in 17th and 18th centuries)

1499	Last of Črnojević family
1499–1697	Tribal chieftains and bishops rule under Ottoman Turks
1697–1735	Bishop Danilo, 1st effective opponent of Turkish rule
1735–1781	Bishop Sava, cautious, timid, gave up power twice
1750–1766	Bishop Vasilije
1767–1773	Šćepan Mali
1782–1830	Bishop Peter I Petrović-Njegoš
1830–1851	Bishop Peter II Petrović-Njegoš
1851–1860	Prince Danilo Petrović-Njegoš, nephew of Peter II
1860–1916	Prince Nikola Petrović

Foreword

The tragic events which led to the break-up of Yugoslavia have demonstrated that, even in this information age, the governments and people of countries not intimately involved in the Balkans were and still are mostly uniformed about that part of the world.

Alex Dragnich, a highly regarded scholar who has written a great deal about Serbia and the Serbs throughout his distinguished academic career has undertaken the very timely task of writing a brief history of Serbia hoping that the dissolution of Yugoslavia not only be better understood but also more objectively evaluated. Unfortunately, during the past dozen years, U.S. policy and American media coverage were mostly anti-Serb. The break-up of Yugoslavia was invariably described as Serb intransigence; the wars that were fought were more often than not blamed on Serb aggression; the murders and rapes that occurred were almost always described as having been committed by Serbs.

While the Serbs were, of course, not blameless, there were many actors and perpetrators other than Serbs in this tragedy. It is plain that had the policy makers and the media been better informed about Balkan and particularly Serb history, governmental actions and editorial conclusions would have been different. Hopefully, this book will help prevent future miscalculations and, very importantly, lead to some reassessment of recent policies and media opinion.

Walter R. Roberts
Former Counselor of the
American Embassy in Yugoslavia

Introduction

My purpose in writing this picture of Serbia's history is two-fold: (1) a hope that recent developments in the wake of Yugoslavia's break-up can be better understood, and (2) more objectively evaluated. Unfortunately, during the past dozen years, United States policy and American media coverage was mostly anti-Serb. The dissolution of Yugoslavia was invariably ascribed to Serb intransigence, that the wars that were fought were more often than not blamed on Serb aggression; the murders and rapes that occurred were almost always described as having been committed by Serbs.

Not only are these things not correct, but it is also plain that had the policy makers and the media been better informed about Balkan and particularly Serbian history, conclusions and actions may have been very different. Hopefully the chapters that follow will prevent future mistakes and, very importantly, lead to some reassessment of recent policies and media coverage.

But getting to the truth is not easy. The Serbs are an ancient people. Their experiences through the ages have often been distorted or mistreated. Lies about Serbs vary from the type of good-natured jibe, for example, by a psychology professor seeking to provoke his freshman class with the declaration "ninety percent of what you know isn't so," to those who don't know the difference. A professor friend of mine, for example, believed that our boundary with Canada had been determined by the declaration "fifty-four forty or fight" (a claim that was actually settled at the 49th degree of latitude). And there are those who are perfectly happy to make lies of the "whole cloth." And then there are those in between, motivated by different reasons. There are the lazy ones who grab what they get from others. And there are those who like to rush to judgment without thinking about the consequences world-wide of misguided actions by the United States.

Aside from my brief treatment of Serbia's early history (medieval Serbia) and the long years of Ottoman rule over the Serbs (nearly five hundred years), I begin with the initial Serb uprising of 1804. After that, twin evolving political streams move throughout the century: (1)

the gradual liberating from Ottoman rule and the replacement of that authority by Serbs, and (2) the determined efforts by Serbs to limit their own rulers in such a way that eventually the result would be a parliamentary democracy, which was accomplished by the end of the century. In the twentieth century, the Serbs joined other South Slavs in the First and Second Yugoslavias, with the latter collapsing in the last decade of the century.

Now, the Serbs of Serbia and Montenegro face a new future.

I

Creating and Building the State: Medieval Serbia

This chapter will seek to describe Medieval Serbia, i.e., the main events and developments from the arrival of the Serbs on the Balkan Peninsula to their loss of the Battle of Kosovo to the Turks in 1389 and the extinction of the state soon after.

The ancient beginnings of any people are shrouded in uncertainty. Nevertheless, there is some agreement among historians that the Serbs, along with other South Slavic tribes, moved westward from the general area of the Carpathian Mountains to the Balkan Peninsula somewhere between the 6th and 9th centuries. They occupied territories roughly on a line from the southern Adriatic Sea to the central part of today's Serbia. Put in other words, they moved into areas that had been occupied by the Romans and the Byzantines. Eventually, they moved slightly eastward to present-day Kosovo, which was to become the center of medieval Serbia.

Serbia, originally known as Rascia or Raška, found itself in the midst of the mighty Byzantine Empire. The Serbs benefited from the empire's internal weaknesses and from the attacks of the Crusades from the West. The Crusades came through Serbia's Morava valley. Serbia's first noted ruler was Nemanja, whose heirs were to succeed him. Nemanja personally met the leader of the Third Crusade, Barbarossa, in 1189.

Parenthetically, it might be noted that this Serbian encounter with the Crusaders would come to haunt them centuries later when they began to attribute some of their major troubles to the great powers using Serbia as a passage way in their expansionist programs. To which a less than sympathetic observer is supposed to have retorted: "No one forced you to build your house in the middle of the road."

Going back to history: Constantinople, which was regarded as the cultural capital of the known world, was captured by the Crusaders in 1204 and the Byzantine Empire broken up into three parts. From then on, Serbia grew and for about 100 years was the strongest empire in the Balkans.

After a defeat by the Byzantines, which was a serious setback, Nemanja obtained political recognition from the West and a crown for his son Stefan. A royal papal delegation delivered the crown in 1207. In 1261, Byzantine leaders recaptured Constantinople, but the restored empire lacked its former strength. And Serbia continued to grow and to prosper. In some ways the most colorful of the Nemanjić rulers was Tsar Dušan (1331–1355). He conquered roughly half of Byzantium and made Serbia the strongest empire in the Balkans. Serbia's territory in Dušan's time covered vast areas from the Danube, the lower Adriatic, and the Aegean. Dušan signed his edicts: "Emperor and Autocrat of the Serbs, Byzantines, Bulgars, and Albanians."

Dušan did not hide his claim to the throne of Byzantium. He wanted the powerful Greek clergy in Byzantium to recognize him. When they refused, he called the Serbian and Bulgarian bishops together, who raised the autonomous Serbian archbishopric to the rank of Patriarchate (1346), and in less than a month the newly-elected Serbian Patriarch crowned him emperor. Dušan subjugated the center of Byzantine Christianity—Mount Athos. Apart from Constantinople, Athos was the most active spiritual and cultural center of Byzantium. Dušan traveled to visit the Serbian monastery, Hilandar, together with his wife Jelena, the latter a feat in itself because no female (human *or* animal) was ever permitted to set foot on the peninsula of Mount Athos. But apparently Jelena heeded the warning of the Blessed Mother and did not go into the monastery itself.

Most of Dušan's imperial time was spent in the Hellenic area of his realm. Knowing Greek, he felt pretty much at home there, leaving central Serbia in the care of his son Uroš. He courted the West, hoping to get help to take Constantinople, but his pleas were rejected. Even though he was defending Christianity, the Roman Catholic rulers saw him as foreign to their faith. But Dušan was so determined that he was even willing to cast aside his wife and to marry a Western princess, but even this was not enough to get him a few naval vessels for his plan to conquer Constantinople. What would have happened, we do not know, because time ran out for him with his untimely death in 1355. The rule of his successors was anti-climatic and, as we know, the Ottoman Turks defeated Serbia in 1389, followed by the end of the state shortly thereafter.

To better understand Serbia and the Serbs, it would help to have a brief description of the major institutions of medieval Serbia. The major subjects to be treated forthwith will include: (1) political authority and institutions; (2) religion, mainly the acceptance of Christianity and its impact; and (3) Serbia's relations with its neighbors.

Political Authority and Institutions

In medieval Serbia political authority centered on a monarch, usually having the title of tsar, although the title of prince, king, and emperor were also employed. There were also assemblies, but they did not have the power to legislate or limit the powers of the monarch. Most of the available evidence suggests that the members of assemblies came from the nobility and the higher clergy. Although it was nowhere decreed who had the right to participate, the assemblies at times appeared as broad national meetings. The monarch decided whom to call and when, indicating that they were advisory bodies. No doubt, members of the ruler's family and close friends, as well as his major military commanders, were intimate advisers. There is no evidence of debates in the assemblies.

In terms of social structure, the Serbia of the middle ages had developed into a type of feudal society. There were classes and there were privileged elements. It is important to note, however, that classes were not yet organized and that there were no class assemblies. It appears that the rulers granted special privileges only when circumstances forced them to do so. We should note that when Serbia was resurrected in the nineteenth century there were no classes.

The assemblies were called together to assist in the selection of the church head, to hear proclamations from the ruler, or to witness his installation as the monarch. Sometimes they were called to advise on various administrative questions. Serbian assemblies often seemed to have a church-state character because they dealt with religious as well as state matters. Unlike in the West, the Serbian church did not use natural law to put the church above the state. Moreover, the Serbian clergy did not gather the nobility around itself as a way of limiting the monarch's authority, but as a way of becoming the ruler's strongest supporters and the guardian of national unity. Cooperation instead of hostility seemed to characterize Serbian assemblies. The churches helped to create a sense of national identity, which was to be critical during the long years of Turkish rule after the fall of the state.

On paper, the greatest political heritage of medieval Serbia was Tsar Dušan's Law Code, studiously prepared over a period of about six years (1349–1354). It is recognized to be among the leading law systems in the world. This code was an independent Serbian creation, although it may have borrowed or adapted certain rules from Byzantine law. The Code is a combination of public and private law, seeking to regularize and systematize social and economic relations. It seeks to protect the rights of the peasants as well as the nobility. It included penalties, among other things, for homicides, arson, theft, bribery, drunkenness, swearing, and counterfeiting. It also laid down rules for judges and for the clergy.

When Serbia regained its independence from the Turks in the nineteenth century, and set about developing its own judicial institutions, it is not altogether clear to what extent Dušan's Code was a source. We do know that Matija Nenadović, one of the most learned men of the time, was given the task of drafting laws for the resurrected state. He had a copy of Justinian's Code and he was familiar with the Mosaic Law. In his memoirs he does not mention Dušan's Code, but a noted Serbian scholar who wrote about ancient Serbian law insists that Nenadović borrowed more from Dušan's Code than any other.

Religion: Conversion to Christianity

Perhaps the most impressive heritage of medieval Serbia, certainly the most physically visible in the Serbs' conversion to Christianity, are the many churches and monasteries that were build. When the Serbs came to the Balkan Peninsula, they brought with them some religious beliefs but were also ready to accept new ways. From our present view, Serb society was rather primitive, but evolving and fumbling for paths to a more desirable way of life. And Christianity seems to have had a powerful attraction. It was like a bombshell. Most important, it captured the imagination of the Serbian rulers who became dedicated to the building of churches and monasteries. Each ruler believed that he should build at least one church. Some rulers built more than one. According to some Serbian writers, at one time there were over one thousand churches, with approximately 20 major ones. It is important to note that the claim of large numbers of churches needs some qualification. Many were what Serbs called "Brvnare," a little like cabins made of wood, with scant attributes of churches, perhaps a cross or two.

Despite centuries of neglect during the subsequent Turkish occupation, many of the churches and monasteries were remarkably well preserved, and testify in some degree to the cultural level that the Serbs had achieved. At least two of the monasteries were proclaimed world art treasures by international scholars after the Second World War. Countless churches and monasteries were destroyed or damaged by the Kosovo Albanians after the NATO powers occupied the area in 1999.

Christian religious beliefs and behavior thus became the overwhelming underpinning of Serbian society. Unlike rulers in Western Europe, Serbian ones left a heritage of monasteries instead of huge and elaborate castles. It is instructive to note that the youngest son of the first of the line of the Nemanja rulers, Sava (better known as Saint Sava), who was to become the first real head of the Serbian Orthodox Church, took a secret path to Mount Athos and became a monk. Even more dramatic was the decision of the father to give up his throne and join Sava as a monk.

The monasteries were more than religious institutions; they were also cultural and educational centers. There is also some evidence that the monasteries were centers of economic life as well as political centers. The latter can be said particularly about those monasteries that were heavily fortified. The building of some monasteries was probably politically motivated, as a way of tying the church and state together, i.e., strengthening the latter.

We do not know precisely when the Serbs converted to Christianity. By the end of the ninth century certain missionaries were at work in the Balkans. These were the pupils of the missionaries who had been sent to Moravia from Byzantium. The notable ones were Cyril and Methodius. It is believed that they converted the Serbs. Each Serb celebrates the day when it is thought that his ancient ancestors first accepted Christianity. This is known as the *Slava*, which was passed on from one generation to the next, from father to son. The *Slava* is unique among the Slavs. When a Serbian woman marries she celebrates her husband's *Slava*.

World art historians have praised the architecture of the monasteries and especially the interiors with their beautifully decorated frescoes. They have singled out several for special praise. The monastery
Studenica is one of these, with its frescoes, carvings and ornaments in
marble, and painted scenes of the life of Christ and the saints. Another
is the monastery Mileševo, whose frescoes have actual portraits of
Saint Sava and his nephew, and a depiction of the angel at the tomb of
Christ. There are hues and nuances in the colors as well as the lavish
use of gold in the background. Still another is the monastery Sopoćani,
which has a place of honor in any survey of European arts in the thir-
teenth century. The monastery Gračanica, on the field of Kosovo, is
praised for the depth of its scenery and its attention to detail in the
storytelling of each depicted event, such as faithfully reproducing the
shapes of eating utensils, and food and costumes.

When we move to the mid-fourteenth century, we have the monastery Dečani, that superb legacy of King Stefan Dečanski and his son
Dušan, which contains no less than one thousand iconographic scenes.
The monastery was completed by 1348, a time when Dušan had already
proclaimed himself "Emperor of Serbs and Greeks." The supernatural
size of Dušan's portrait and the beautifully executed family-tree of the
Nemanjić dynasty as a counterpart to the genealogy of Christ show the
opulence and richness of life that was visible not only in the ruler's
court but had also spread to many of his noblemen.

Some have observed that not only are the monasteries tangible
evidence of the conversion of Serbs to Christianity, but in addition, in
an era when reading and writing were not widespread and were
restricted to a relatively small number of persons, the frescoes and
manuscripts with illuminations served as tools for the transmission of
religious teachings as well as a reminder of the content of those teachings. The painted walls of churches and chapels in the monasteries truly
served as the Bible of the poor and illiterate populace.

In addition to the monasteries on Serbian soil, mention should be
made of some monuments outside Serbia, notably the monastery
Hilandar on Mount Athos in Greece, founded by Nemanja and Saint
Sava, with its church rebuilt by Milutin and enlarged by Prince Lazar.
To this day it serves as a cultural center for Serbs, and has always
served as a beacon for Serbs everywhere.

The first significant document of Serbian literacy is a Christian book—the Gospels of Miroslav, dating from the latter half of the twelfth century. It is an enormously important document because it not only represents the work of a literary scribe who could both read and write, but it also implies that it was written for persons who could read the script and understand the meaning of the text, which was translated from the original Greek. This precious parchment contains fascinating miniature paintings at the beginnings of many paragraphs of the text. It also signifies that in living side by side with more advanced cultures—Byzantine and Western—the Serbs were accepting the idea of written transmission of documents.

Cultural Activity Outside the Church

Medieval Serbia, starting from scratch, made significant progress with the printed word. They were assisted in various ways. Mention has already been made of the Greek priests, Cyril and Methodius. They played the primary role in the construction of an alphabet and a script for the Serbs, adapted from the Greek.

There is evidence of Serbian literary creations, poems and other writings as early as the late eleventh and the beginning of the twelfth centuries. The earliest writings appear to be books needed for religious services in the growing number of churches and monasteries. A great many were translations from the Greek.

In addition, there were a number of biographies. Perhaps the earliest was Saint Sava's biography of his father, Nemanja, the founder of the Serbian dynasty and of Serbian statehood. He titled it *The Life of Master Simeun*. In addition to a profusion of translated church manuals, canonic and instructive texts for use by Serbian monks and priests, Sava also tried his hand at verse writing. Being the most traveled Serb of his time, Sava visited and personally knew several Byzantine emperors, as well as the patriarchs of Constantinople. Sava's brother, King Stefan the First-Crowned (1196–1228) also wrote a biography of his father. Being occupied with matters of state, he wrote from the point of view of a dynast, national ruler, protector of the faith and statesman. Subsequently, a new generation of Serbian authors wrote about Nemanja, Sava, and King Stefan. The early biographies tended to be personal. Subsequent ones added geographical descriptions and ethnographic data, as well as references to historical events of the period.

Prince Lazar's son, Despot Stefan (1389–1427), the last of medieval Serbia's rulers, was a great benefactor, protector of refugees, writers and artists. He was an author in his own right. One of his poetic scripts is entitled, "Love Surpasses Everything, and No Wonder Because God is Love." Another was the "Ode to Prince Lazar," a beautiful text chiseled in the marble column that was placed at the spot of the Battle of Kosovo.

Among medieval Serbia's patriarchs, the best of the literati was Danilo III (Elected at the Council of Žiča, 1390), who together with Lazar's widow and her children, transported the body of the beheaded Prince from Kosovo to the Ravanica Monastery and canonized Lazar to Sainthood.

Through contacts with the South Adriatic littoral, some great literary works came to Serbia in translation. Among these are the Tales of India, the story of Tristan and Isolde, stories of Alexander the Great, and the story of the Trojan War.

The various writings were initially copied by hand on parchment and later on paper when it became available for this purpose. The first Serbian printing press came into existence in Obod, near Cetinje in Montenegro, producing the first book (liturgical poetry) in 1494. We should note that the first printing press with movable type was invented by Guttenberg in Germany in the 1440s.

Serbia and its Neighbors

Medieval Serbia was also part of the international community at that time. Travel routes across Serbia linked East and West. Three famous Byzantine writers (Theodore Metohit, Nikifor Grigor, and Jovan Kantakuzin) spent briefer or longer periods of time in Serbia, and their writings contain information about Serbian lands, people, and state.

In political, military, and cultural matters, Serbian royal courts communicated on levels of respect and honor with Venetian Doges, Hungarian Kings, Bulgarian Tsars, and Byzantine Emperors. Moreover, they were connected with most of them through marital arrangements. The first wife of Stefan the First-Crowned was Eudocia, daughter of Byzantine Emperor Alexis III. Serbian King Stefan Uroš I married the French princess Helene (House of Anjou), and Stefan Dragutin married Katherine, daughter of Hungarian King Stephen V.

The long reign of Milutin (1282–1321) witnessed much domestic and foreign activity. It was during his rule that Saxon miners came to Serbia, constituting the beginning of organized exploitations of mines of various ores, particularly silver, which was used for coins and for jewelry. Coins were actually minted before the arrival of professional miners, who also brought with them special legal codes for miners. The earliest Serbian coins were apparently those of Radoslav in the late 1220s.

With new arrivals, a mining center was developed in Novo Brdo, where gold was discovered. Novo Brdo grew, and by the middle of the fifteenth century it was a city of about 40,000 inhabitants. It was the largest city in Serbian lands, as well as the largest mining settlement in all of Europe.

Medieval Serbia, the Serbia of the Nemanjić Dynasty, was without a doubt a land of economic and cultural progress that surpassed the European average. Apart from the well-known monasteries and their impressive frescoes, there are smaller but masterful art objects from that era: golden cups and chalices, candlesticks and silver plates, jeweled reliquaries, delicate embroideries, book bindings, and artistic illuminations—produced by a talented people in a society that gave them opportunities to express themselves. As for Serbian rulers, they did not seek to imitate those in the West who built magnificent castles, but committed most of their money and their talent to building Houses of God.

II

Serbia Under Foreign Rule

A nation disappears; 400 years later it reappears. A fairytale headline? Not at all. The resurrection was real. Such is the history of Serbia from its defeat at Kosovo by the Ottoman Turks in 1389 to the First Serbian Uprising in 1804. Most Serbs have viewed those 415 years as a dark age in which the glories of Serbia's medieval legacy were erased only to be rekindled in the rise of modern Serbia. That period is the story of endurance, patience, and courage of a people under two strong empires—the Ottoman and the Habsburg—who managed to survive and rearise as a proud nation. The story of that survival is not easily portrayed because it involved many developments—social, political, economic, and cultural—which not only involved the Serbs with those empires, but also with Venice and other European nations. A number of recent studies lend various insights into how the Serbs managed to survive as a people and once again emerge as a nation after centuries of foreign rule.

Without a state and without any type of communications to connect them, the Serbs in various regions faced local conditions as best as they could. Other than the use of infrequent Tatar couriers, even the Turkish *vezirs* did not have ways of communicating with the capital, Constantinople, or with other Turkish governors. Under the existing conditions the destinies of the Serbs can be classified under four general approaches: vassalage and autonomy; military service; migration and emigration; and the role of the Serbian Orthodox Church and Serbian epic poetry in maintaining a national identity. These are not exclusive because the Ottoman Empire exercised different degrees of control in different parts of its realm, and the Serbs also exhibited varying talents and skills of accommodating to the changed circumstances.

In order to understand the development of vassalage and autonomy, it is necessary to remember that after the defeat at Kosovo, the Serbian state, nobility, and political institutions did not disintegrate immediately. This came about in part from the confusion after Kosovo because the Turkish Sultan was also killed. In the south, some of the Serbian nobility accepted the new Sultan's rule while retaining control over their lands and privileges in return for loyalty and military service. Tsar Lazar's son and successor, Stefan Lazarević, became a vassal prince. The Sultan's death in 1403 resulted in strife about the succession, which allowed Lazarević to restore a part of the territorial integrity and independence of his domain. Subsequently, the Turks restored their authority, and by the 15th century the independence of Lazarević was whittled away.

Generally, Ottoman administration was not as oppressive as other states of Europe. German historian Leopold Ranke wrote that Serbia prospered, especially in stock raising. Moreover, he says that Hadzi Musthafa was so well-intentioned that the people called him "the Serbian mother." As mentioned above, the Ottoman's main interest was in maintaining its revenues and military forces. Most of the subjects of the Sultan were ruled indirectly through *feudatories* who were granted land and peasants to till it in return for military service. These feudatories provided the main cavalry forces for the Sultan.

In addition, the Ottomans divided the empire's subjects according to religious affiliation, giving the religious leaders some authority in civil government. The different ethno-religious groups had their own courts within their respective areas. With the breakdown of central authority in the 16th century and after, due to rapacious local governors, greedy landowners, freebooting soldiers and corrupt tax officials, Ottoman authority became more oppressive believing that its revenues and free movement of its armed forces were threatened.

In the long run, most Serbs who were peasants came under direct Ottoman rule. Yet most Serbs and other Christian subjects, if they paid their taxes and fulfilled their feudal obligations, were in considerable measure left to themselves. The extended patriarchal family, the *zadruga*, the clan, and tribe, in some areas provided a measure of solidarity and a sense of belonging which helped to weather the hardships of foreign rule. In some areas the local prince (*knez*), the assembly, and local church were able to retain some autonomy.

Not only were Serbs scattered in different parts of the empire, their political, legal and social conditions varied considerably. Often the Serbs found themselves juxtaposed between the rising Ottoman Empire and the powerful Hungarian kingdom. The latter often granted the Serbs privileges in return for their willingness to help in the defense of the empire. The Serbs attempted to perform a balancing act as a way of preserving some autonomy, at times aligning themselves with the Hungarians and at other times with the Ottomans.

The development of self-governing institutions on the village level, and the separate legal system of the Serbian Orthodox Church made possible a limited amount of autonomy in many areas. Because of location and military service, certain communities were able to retain even more autonomy from Ottoman rule. Montenegro's social organization based upon a tribal system, its geographic advantage, its proximity to areas under Venetian control, and the skill of its soldiers, gave them *de facto* independence by the 18th century.

Military service was also a factor in Serbian survival and the maintenance of bits of autonomy. The Serbs were prized as soldiers both by the Habsburgs and the Ottomans. In addition to the Islamized Serbian boys who were impressed into the *Jannisary* corps, many Serbs served in the Ottoman armed forces without having to give up their religion. For that service, they were able to retain their land holdings and were free of taxation. Some armed Serbs engaged in banditry and other rebellious acts, which brought Ottoman reprisals. From among the Christian boys serving in the Sultan's palace guard, however, some rose to high positions, including Grand Vizier.

The Serbs also served in the military forces of other countries. The Kingdom of Naples recruited Serbs. Following the end of the Serbian Despotate of Smederevo in 1459, the Hungarian king provided Serbs some lands in return for their military service. For a time the Serbs made up an important segment of the Black Legion, the king's standing army. With the defeat of the Hungarians at Mohacs (1526), however, the Hungarian Serb Despotate ended.

In some ways, the most important military service for the Serbs was their service in Russian armies as early as the late 16th and early 17th centuries as cavalrymen along with other Balkan troops. With the rise of Russia as a European power under Peter the Great and his successors, military and political relations between Russia and Serbia intensified. The Serbs organized and participated in uprising against the Ottomans during the Russo-Turkish wars of the 18th and early 19th centuries.

The Serbs fought for the United States in its first foreign war. This was against the Barbary pirates in 1805. General William Eaton utilized a mixed company of Serbs and Greeks, commanded by Serbian Captain

Luka Ulović (Luca Ulovix) in the conflict. Together with twelve U.S. marines, the Serbian-led Balkan troops captured the fortress of Derna.

Military service also took Serbs to other parts of Europe. In a number of events it could be said that there was an important link between Serbian military service and their survival. From the 16th through the 19th century, the Habsburg Empire organized what they called the military frontier. The purpose was to protect its crownlands from Ottoman military threats, which twice besieged Vienna. To man the frontier, the Austrians encouraged the settlement of Serbs as farmer-soldiers with grants of land and other privileges. The Serbs were also mobilized in formations known as *Freikorps*, especially during various Austro-Turkish wars. Many from the ranks of Serbs in the *Freikorps* were found in the First Serbian Uprising of 1804 against the Turks, including their leader, Karadjordje.

A critically important aspect of the Serbs' activity while under Ottoman rule were the migrations. These took place mainly in the second half of the 17th century and the first half of the 18th century. This was a period of migrations, of continuous mobility. The migrations were often led by church leaders. The most noted example was the large Serbian exodus, led by Patriarch Arsenije III Črnojević, who led 30,000 Serbian families. Eventually, the total number of refugees reached about 200,000. Another migration, led by Patriarch Arsenije IV came in 1736–1739. It is necessary to mention the reasons, the opportunities, and the consequences of the migrations.

The principal reason was the unbearable anti-Serb actions of the Albanians. When the Serbs fell under Ottoman control, the great majority of the Kosovo Albanians were Christian, and relations between them were cordial and even friendly. But by the 17th century, Islamization among the Albanians was a huge success. Islamization among the Serbs was basically a failure, mainly because the Serbs had Kosovo, while the Albanians had no similar spiritual anchor.

Fortunately, opportunities for the Serbs to escape the Albanian hostilities became available. Around the beginning of the 17th century, German commanders of the Austrian border areas (today's Slavonia and Croatia) were luring Christian peasants from Serbia and Bosnia to settle in the vacant but fertile areas, and to "fight for the Cross." This whole region was considered a military district, under the administration of the Vienna government, and was exempt from any other authority. The new settlers were promised a great deal of autonomy, religious freedom, and free election of their local chiefs. Local feudal lords liked the idea of protecting their lands, but not at the price of losing their local benefits. The new settlers, mostly Serbs, did not want to abide by any orders of the feudal lords, and the military commanders sided with them.

On the other hand, while the Ottoman authorities did not like to see settlers moving away, in the end for every Christian who moved out of the Balkan area, they brought in an Albanian. In a sense, by inviting the Christian Serbs to cross the river, Austria was de-Christianizing the Balkans. The Albanians were happy to see the Serbs move north. Consequently, the Islamization of Slav territories went steadily onward. Serbian historians and ethnographers have described in detail the various routes of Serbian migrations.

A significant part of the Serbs sought refuge in the forested hill country of Serbia (Šumadija), the mountainous regions of Bosnia-Herzegovina, Montenegro, and the Danube and Sava river valleys. In some ways Montenegro was the most important because it was never fully subjugated by the Turks. The Serbs also settled in lands that were nominally within the Ottoman Empire, but where the authority of the latter was weak or non-existent. These communities maintained their self-rule through their clan or tribal organizations. The Ottomans found it difficult and costly to subdue these communities.

The *zadruga*, a Serbian familial organization, defined by most sociologists as an "extended family," provided the Serbs a sort of collective security blanket. In some ways it was like a local peasant commune, or a state in miniature. The *zadruga* organized family activities and provided a solid backbone for morals and religion. In times of danger, it assisted in the common defense. In recent times, the term *zadruga* was used to describe a cooperative.

Many Serbs who migrated to Austrian and Venetian lands prospered. Moreover, they came into contact with the growing commerce and culture of Europe, and began to take part in the economic, political, and cultural changes affecting Europe. A Serbian commercial class and Serbian communities began to develop in such centers as Novi Sad, Vienna, Trieste, and Constantinople, among others.

The South Slavs of Dalmatia and Slovenia were the most affected by European developments of the sixteenth century. In the course of the fifteenth century, Venice had again gained control of the coast, with the exception of Dubrovnik, but this did not curb the increasingly Slav character of Dalmatia because of the inflow of refugees due to endemic warfare thereafter between the Turkish hinterland and the Venetian shore. The Dubrovnik Republic remained both independent and neutral. Dubrovnik was well placed to act as an intermediary between the developing manufacturers of Europe and their markets in the East.

Some Serbs who engaged in overland and overseas trade between Europe and the Ottoman Empire accumulated wealth and built churches, schools, and publishing houses in their native and adopted lands. It was in this environment that modern Serbian nationalism was born. But all of these positive developments were countered by the negative factors discussed above.

In some ways, the most important factor in the survival of the Serbian people after Kosovo was the Serbian Orthodox Church. Most Serbian political and cultural institutions disintegrated in the long years after the defeat at Kosovo. But the Church was the one institution that preserved and perpetuated elements of Serbia's great historical past. Ironically, the Serbs were assisted by the Ottoman tolerance toward other religions so long as their flocks exhibited a basic loyalty toward the sultan.

Oddly enough, two brothers played key roles in directly helping the Serbs. One, Mehmed Sokoli, was of Serb origin who had risen to Grand Vizier under the Sultan. Due to his intervention the Serbian Orthodox Patriarchate was established in 1556. His brother, Makarije Sokolović, became patriarch. Previously under the Greek Patriarch of Constantinople, the Serbian Patriarch was now recognized as independent within the Ottoman Empire. And its ecclesiastical authority went beyond the boundaries of the Serbian medieval state.

As long as the Ottoman state was prosperous and Ottoman rule relatively benign, the Serbian Church was satisfied to maintain its loyalty to the Ottomans. When the Ottoman authorities experienced internal and external disorders, however, their rule became abusive. This prompted some of the Serbian priests to get involved in insurrectional activities. As mentioned earlier, Turkish abuses also led to Serbian migrations. The Ottoman response was to abolish the autonomy of the Serbian Patriarchate in 1755, leaving it again under the Greek Patriarchate of Constantinople. The result was that in Ottoman territory the Serbian clergy and laity had to struggle against both Greek and Ottoman dominance. The metropolitanate of Sremski Karlovci, which had been an offshoot of the Patriarchate of Peć, took up the leadership of Serbs in Hungary and other areas not under the Ottomans.

Nevertheless, the best of the Serbian Church rose to the task of carrying out its inspirational role to a remarkable degree. A nation brutally beaten, a nation enslaved, a nation beheaded of leadership, and robbed of literacy, turned to its primitive monks and national bards. As if unimpressed by the enormity of their task, they suddenly found themselves being a depository and source of national hope. The monasteries as religious centers suddenly became national centers.

Ill-equipped and inexperienced, and scared to death, the patriarchs seated at the Peć Monastery indeed served their nation. In tough periods they stood their ground until chased away. But even in migrations they carried out their mission. They still wore their ecclesiastical robes; they always wore the signs of priestly dignity—censers, crosses and shepherd's rods. The Serbian people, however, did not bow to them as sextons, but as rulers. In enslaved Serbia, the patriarch was not a clergyman, but judge, administrator, historian, and teacher—everything that the priest was not in free Serbia. And when the Serbs kissed his hand, they did not do so out of reverence or faith, but out of the respect which is shown to the leader of the nation. And so the patriarch became more of a leader and less of a shepherd. He continued to wear the cross, but the Serbs looked to the hand that held the national seal.

The Serbian Church tended to lose its dogmatic character and increasingly accepted an ethnic character. It became an integral part of the national spirit, just as folklore is an integral part of that spirit.

Fortunately, in the most trying times for the Serbs, the second center of Serbianism, Montenegro, was able to pick up the fallen Serbian standard. Regardless of how tiny a lighthouse, Montenegro was the last remaining Serbian beacon, and it was important for several reasons. First, it meant that the light had not been extinguished. Second, it had a powerful Slav provider, Moscow. Third, it was not an Austrian territory. Fourth, it was in the immediate vicinity of Turkish and Albanian Islamism. And last but not least, Montenegrin leaders had not for a moment abandoned the ideal of Serbia's resurrection.

The head of the Serbian Orthodox Church in Montenegro, the Vladika (Prince-Bishop) of Montenegro, was not only the head of the Church but also of the state. That church played an unusual role in the preservation of Serbian national identity and in getting Serbs to connect with Serbia's medieval past, especially the veneration of Serbian saints and other leaders of whom the Serbs could be proud. One result was that along with the Greeks, the Serbs had the most well-developed ethnic identity in the Balkans and this at the time of the emergence of modern nationalism in Europe in the late 18th and early 19th centuries.

Serbian epic poetry was interrelated with the role of the Church in linking the Serbian past to later generations. Those poems maintained the memory of deeds of heroism at a time when histories were not being written down. The most famous cycle of this poetry was the Kosovo Cycle, recounting the monumental battle for Serbian freedom and the need to struggle and sacrifice to safeguard liberty. Some writers have compared the remembrances of Serbia's glorious past to the Homeric epic poems that served similar purposes for the Greeks.

The poems spoke of deeds of valor and martial virtues. They told of suffering and sacrifice of Serbs, as they were scattered to many places. Together with the Serbian Orthodox Church, the epic poems built a Serbian national awareness that developed and articulated a national movement. They helped to maintain a religious and historical identity of Serbs in the long centuries after Kosovo. The Church inculcated a sense of belonging to a faith that was distinct from Islam and Catholicism, but also different from the Orthodoxy as practiced by other Eastern Christians.

The epic poetry preserved a sense of Serbian history in an era where literary and written records were almost non-existent. In this way the moral and ethical elements of Serbia's medieval legacy and Serbian religious customs were particularly important in the formation of the more modern Serbian national identity.

The above discussion does not explain the whole historical experience of the Serbs in the period 1389–1804, but it does provide us with a context in which to understand the complex story of Serbia's survival. It should help us to appreciate the Serbian story of those years as one of sacrifice, fortitude, and patience—years in which they endured more than 400 years of foreign rule and in the end emerged anew as a free nation.

III
Serb Uprisings: 1804–1815

The Serbia of 1804 was not the Serbia of 1389. Nearly 500 years of Ottoman rule had wrought many changes. Yet these were far less than might have been expected. Amazing as it might seem, the Serbs could still think of themselves as Serbs. Perhaps the greatest credit should go to the Serbian Orthodox Church. In some ways the most impressive heritage of medieval Serbia are its monasteries, certainly they are the most physically visible. At one time there were over 20 major ones and many minor ones. Despite centuries of neglect during the Turkish occupation, many of these were remarkably well preserved. Aside from what the monasteries did for the Serbs, they testify to us, to some degree, the cultural level that the Serbs had attained.

The monasteries were more than religious institutions. In a limited way, they were also cultural and educational centers. The political importance of the monasteries in the period of Turkish rule was twofold. First, they were and continued to be symbols of national identity. Second, they were places where in a small way the clergy could get some education, enabling the priests to pass on, in oral communication, something of Serbia's historical and cultural heritage. They conveyed to the people the idea that the Serbian nation had a religious mission, that it was difficult to think of a free church without a truly independent country.

The heritage of the nation's greatness was also perpetuated by talented people in folk tales, songs, and legends. Moreover, many Serbs who lived abroad (in Montenegro, Austria, and Hungary) devoted their intellectual efforts toward the preservation of Serbian national identity. They also worked toward the realization of Serbian independence. And in the 19th century, as Serbia sought to build the nation, many Serbs living in places like Novi Sad, particularly those who were educated in western or central Europe, came to Belgrade to offer their distinctive talents.

The geographic size of the Serbian state in the early years of the 19th century can only be approximated. In 1815 it was about the size of Massachusetts, less than 10,000 square miles. It was considerably increased by 1833. Later in the century, after wars with Turkey, it was about 18,000 square miles. In population, Serbia went from less than 500,000 in 1815 to nearly one million by mid-century. By 1890, the population exceeded two million, and on the eve of World War I, it was approximately 4.5 million.

As already indicated, during the long period of Ottoman rule, Serbs migrated in large numbers, mainly to Hungary and Austria. After 1804 and 1815, many returned, but they also came from Bosnia-Herzegovina and Montenegro. Many were induced to come by grants of free lands and exemption from taxation for up to three years.

At the beginning of the 19th century, Serbia was a rather primitive land. By comparison with Western Europe, there was general backwardness. There was little or no industry. Even in the largest center, Belgrade, glass windows and mirrors were rare, and in the interior they were unknown. Tables and chairs, as well as tableware, were nonexistent or rare. Communications, except for some riverboat traffic, were virtually nonexistent. The general cultural situation was dismal. Schools were scarce, and teachers—most of them by birth were from Austria—were poorly trained. There were no hospitals in 1815, and no certified doctors until 1819. The first pharmacy was opened in 1826.

Stock-raising, which had grown rapidly in the 18th century, was the predominant characteristic of the Serbian economy. In the 19th century land cultivation developed alongside stock-raising. The principal exports consisted of hogs, steers, sheep and wool with some ninety percent going to Austria-Hungary. At the same time, ninety percent of Serbia's imports came from the dual monarchy. This situation was used subsequently by the latter to exert various forms of pressure on Serbia.

In terms of social structure, the Serbs of the middle ages had developed into a type of feudal society, with classes and privileged elements. This structure was destroyed by the long years of Turkish occupation. When Serbia regained its independence in the 19th century, there was no aristocracy or nobility. The resurrected Serbia was in the main a nation of small landowners. There were some more or less well-to-do peasants, Prince Miloš Obrenović among them, who set the future of Serbia during the time of his recognized rule, 1813–1838. He did not permit the establishment of a nobility, and declared the land belonged to him who lived on it.

Many Serbs insist that they would have risen against the Ottomans much earlier had it not been for the foreign policies of the Western great powers, whose relations with the Ottomans were just too cozy to disturb. To be sure, there were hostile actions by Serbs in various localities, but these were always put down by the Empire's authorities. But the uprising in Belgrade in 1804 was a different matter. In point of fact, the revolution was less against Ottoman rule than against local officials who in 1801 had killed the lawful Belgrade Turkish governor, Hadzi Musthafa, who had won a great deal of good will from the Serbs. The local officials imposed a reign of terror, taking away the modest rights of local self-government that the Serbs had acquired in the last decade of the 18th century. The initial aim of the Serb revolt was to restore those privileges. In 1805 the Serbs defeated the Turkish army that was sent against them, forcing the Turks to concede a certain autonomy for Serbia.

This brought on a period of incessant warfare, which ended with the restoration of Ottoman rule in 1813. The leader of the 1804 uprising was Karadjordje (Black George) Petrović. He was chosen in part because of his military experience in the Austrian *Freikorps* and in part because a number of prominent Serbs did not dare put themselves at the head of the revolutionary movement. Soon after the revolt began, political questions arose because many Serbs, including district military commanders, were unhappy with Karadjordje making political decisions. The challenge to his authority was twofold; one was informal, that of district commanders at certain assemblies. The other, more formal, was in the form of an officially created Council.

The idea of the Council seems to have been suggested by the Russian foreign minister to two prominent Serbs who had come to Petrograd seeking Russian assistance against the Turks. The Council was to consist of one representative from each of the twelve districts. It was to have supreme power in the land. In actuality, its powers and functions were never well defined. While it was to limit Karadjordje, any time that it came into conflict with him, his word was sufficient to frustrate its goals and actions.

The struggle for power between Karadjordje and the Council was made more complex by virtue of the fact that the struggle for autonomy had become a struggle for independence. With the latter objective in mind, it was necessary to think of establishing a legal-constitutional order. To this end, some of Karadjordje's opponents were successful in getting a Russian expert, Konstantin K. Rodofinkin, to come to Serbia, avowedly to help Serbia set up an orderly administration. His draft of a constitution would limit Karadjordje's power, but he accepted it because he needed Russia's military assistance, and because he was confident that in practice his powers would not be limited.

The Rodofinkin draft was never implemented because it did not receive the assent of the Russian tsar or that of a Serbian assembly. In its place, Karadjordje and his followers produces an octroyed constitution in December 1810. According to this document, all Serbian military and civil leaders recognized Karadjordje (as well as his lawful descendants) as the supreme leader, to whom all pledged loyalty and allegiance. For his part, Karadjordje promised to exert a fatherly concern for his people, and to recognize the new Council as the supreme court of the land. Moreover, he agreed to issue all orders through the Council and in agreement with it.

In practical terms, the new constitution gave nearly all powers to Karadjordje, while the Council became the administrator of his commands. He was obligated to hear the Council's views but not to accept them. The distrust that continued between the two, and the resumption of the war with Turkey, made that constitution for all practical purposes a dead letter. And by January 1811, Karadjordje was able to reassert his full power, and new constitutional acts confirmed his supremacy. The new Council became a type of central government in which the Prince's supporters and opponents were represented.

One part of the Council became the first Serbian ministry, consisting of six ministers, while the other part of the Council became the supreme court. Together they constituted a type of central authority with legislative powers. Karadjordje was its president. In the struggle with his opponents he had certain advantages. His authoritarianism had the saving grace of representing unity in contrast with the separatism of his political foes. Moreover, the exigencies of war played into his hands. In addition, he placed a number of his actual or potential opponents in subordinate positions, thus separating them from their natural constituencies as well as diluting their powers.

Karadjordje's supremacy, however, was short-lived. Although in the Peace of Bucharest of 1812, Turkey recognized autonomy for Serbia, in 1813 it resumed military operations against Serbia and succeeded in re-establishing its control. Consequently, the Serbian political structure that had evolved did not have an opportunity to prove itself.

Miloš's Serbia, 1815–1838

By 1815, the Turkish political terror was at its height. Following the restoration of Turkish power and the flight of Karadjordje from Serbia, the Turks employed brutal means in an effort to teach the Serbs a lesson. The situation had become so bad by 1815 that leading Serbs were willing to risk everything in an effort to overthrow the Turkish yoke. The revolt was a success, in part because of Russia's intervention. Turkey promised an autonomous administration for Serbia, but that promise was not to be fulfilled for years to come.

Miloš Obrenović, one of the leaders under Karadjordje, had been chosen to lead the revolt in 1815 at the age of 32. He soon realized that it was unrealistic to seek full independence. In stressing his loyalty to the Porte, he made it known that what the Serbs wanted in Belgrade was a decent Turkish governor. More precisely, they wanted Marašli-Ali-paša. In the end, the Turks appointed him and left the matter of Serbian internal affairs to be worked out between Miloš and Marašli-Ali-paša. The agreement reached by the two became the basis of the management of Serbia's internal affairs.

The system of Turkish rule remained. The Serbs, however, made some gains: (1) tax collection was now in the hands of Serbs, (2) local Serbian leaders would take part in court cases involving Serbs, (3) the sum of money for the Turkish governor and his associates would be determined in agreement with national leaders, (4) a council of national leaders would be established in Belgrade. The Serbs thus gained something less than autonomy over a territory roughly half the size of Karadjordje's Serbia.

As the leader of the Serbs, Miloš faced two major tasks—to work for Serbian independence and to create a system of national political authority. In seeking those objectives, he worked on two fronts, the Turkish and the domestic. On the former, national survival was at state, and on the latter, his personal survival. For Miloš, national survival and his own were one and the same thing.

National survival required the nurturing of a precarious identity and working toward increased autonomy, especially in domestic affairs. This necessitated seeking Russian help and counsel while at the same time seeking to assure the Turks of continued Serbian loyalty. To perform this delicate and complicated task, Miloš was sure that he was the only one for the job. Threats to his leadership, therefore, were seen as threats to national survival.

How Miloš sought to achieve his objectives is a long and intricate story. In dealing with the Turks he wanted more autonomy and an expansion of Serbia's territory. In domestic affairs, the Marašli–Miloš agreement could not survive long in practice. Serbian authority grew step by step, in effect replacing Turkish rule. The Turkish governor intended to disarm the Serbs, but it soon became evident that the people could not be disarmed without a serious struggle, and this he did not dare, partly because that might provoke Russia. And Turkish control was not as strong as it appeared. Moreover, Marašli-Ali had learned to live in relative luxury, and he became more and more dependent on Miloš for the money he needed. Lesser Turkish officials were in even more desperate straits, and readily sold themselves to Miloš.

In general, it seems that Miloš had a talent for war and politics. He knew how to handle the sword as well as the purse. In the years 1830–1835, he used a combination of these tactics to get the Turks to recognize him as hereditary prince of Serbia (with dynastic rights for his male heirs), and to add six additional districts to the area of the nation.

Initially, Miloš expanded Serbian authority by ordering district Serbian leaders to perform judicial functions in their areas in cases involving Serbs. He further sought to improve justice by asking judges to use custom and sound reason in reaching their verdicts. In addition, he ordered judges to go to church on Sundays and national holidays, and to fast on Wednesdays and Fridays. And he told them to spend more of their time in courtrooms and less in coffee houses.

Gradually, Miloš succeeded in transforming administrative as well as judicial authority to national elders who were, in fact, his bureaucrats since he appointed them. In this way he became an all-powerful ruler in domestic affairs just as the Turkish governor had been. There was much talk about assemblies (*skupštine*) of elders, but these limited Miloš's authority only to the extent he wanted or permitted. The members of the assemblies were picked by Miloš's civil servants. They met for a day or two when Miloš wanted. From time to time, he felt a need to call them so that he could explain his policies and actions.

The Nature of Miloš's Authority

Miloš became an all-powerful ruler, but he rejected the charge that this was what he wanted. Hearing history read, he said, convinced him that strong rule was the best government when one people "is raising itself from the ruins." He viewed the people as his children and he as their father, likening his authority to that of parental authority over minors. He believed people to be vacillating, unreliable, and easily misled by promises. When angry, he referred to them as an "unthankful bitch" and "livestock without tails."

Initially, Miloš's authority was crude and primitive, but it *was* authority. He was ruthless with his enemies. His fear of domestic opposition resulted in the death of many of his opponents, real or imaginary. In those crimes he saw only preventive measures. Miloš knew of many misdeeds committed by his subordinates and sometimes he took energetic measures against some of his elders, but more often than not he had to ignore their acts because politically he could not do without such men.

In addition to his personal enemies, Miloš had to deal with the outlaws. The large mass of outlaws took on the appearance of a national illness. This could be explained in part as a reaction against taxes and autocratic rule. More important, perhaps, is the fact that many people from various areas had moved into the Belgrade region because it was relatively secure. Many of them had a nomadic and anarchistic character. They had not lived under any systemic state authority and found it difficult to adjust to the order and control of an organized state. The problem of the outlaws was not solved through administrative reforms or liberal policies but by strong and raw repression—by sword and fire. Merciless and barbaric measures were employed, even against families of outlaws. By 1826, the outlaws were virtually eliminated.

Miloš was aware of the type of men around him, but apparently felt helpless. Sometimes he cursed them out unmercifully, and ordered some of them beaten. At the same time he was suspicious of everyone, even his closest officials. He opened their mail and looked through their things. On the whole, however, they served him well. And they were not bound by bureaucratic inertia for the simple reason that there were no established bureaucratic procedures to act as a brake on their actions.

Miloš's Achievements

It is well to summarize Miloš's major achievements. First among them was his getting the Turks in 1830 to recognize him as hereditary prince of Serbia. And while the Porte was only recognizing an already existing situation, and while many viewed it as a selfish act, for Serbia it was a great leap forward.

Second, Miloš succeeded in 1833 to enlarge the Serbian state by adding six districts, nearly doubling the size of the nation. In this case, as with the hereditary principle, Miloš had the support of Russia. In the final stages of gaining the six additional districts, he had to use armed force.

Third, Miloš was successful in establishing order in a fairly primitive society. His methods against the outlaws were brutal and gruesome, but he did establish respect (and fear of) authority. And who is to say that it could have been done with more moderate methods?

Finally, although he became extremely wealthy, Miloš prevented the rise of a landed aristocracy. In the 1830s he refused to reward his associates and friends with lands that were vacated by the Turks. Instead, he divided the land among the peasants. This alienated his erstwhile friends and supporters, who began systematically to undermine his authority.

*   *   *

Generally speaking, the people were not hostile towards Miloš until late in his regime. They knew from experience that it was possible to go from bad to worse. Turkish rule, Karadjordje's rule, and wars were for them as schools of patience. After those experiences, the people seemed to have sensed a need for harmony and unity. Even elders in the society were willing to wait until Miloš had accomplished his basic tasks, and only then to seek security from his arbitrariness.

Early in his regime, Miloš gained the upper hand in relation to other leaders in the country. Before too much time was to pass, he was either appointing district elders or he was placing other men over them so as to reduce their status to that of ordinary bureaucrats. By the end of 1820, the main elders were mostly his brothers, other relatives, or friends. Pursuant to the Marašli–Miloš agreement, the Serbs were allowed to have an office of their own in Belgrade. This was called the National

Chancellery (*Narodna Kancelarija*), which was supposed to be the supreme administrative and judicial organ, made up of 12 *knezes*. But Miloš did not want it to become a governing body, and he did not allow it to become a representative body. It became his personal chancellery, and it went with him wherever he traveled. Through his secretaries, Miloš gave orders and made decisions from which there was no appeal. Miloš's authority was crude and primitive, but it was authority. He seems to have felt that power had to be made visible concretely in the form of a despot before the people could later view it abstractly, independent of the personal wielders of power. This concept could probably have been tolerated until about 1830. What Miloš seems to have failed to comprehend was the need to organize and systematize power. Any such effort—any written laws even—he viewed as diminution of his power.

And Miloš welcomed the intervention of Russia and Austria-Hungary, enemies of constitutions in their lands, because he did not wish to see his power limited by the Council or a parliament.

Following the abolition of the 1835 constitution, Serbia was really without a constitution until 1838. In those years, Miloš's rivals were becoming the favorites of the Porte. At the same time, Miloš prepared one constitutional project after another, only to have it rejected by Russia. Other constitutional projects suggested by foreign powers were not to Miloš's liking. Not really wanting a constitution, Miloš was prepared to accept one only if it gave him the preponderance of power. But the constitution that was forced on Serbia in 1838, by means of another Turkish *hatisherif*, was far from being such a constitution.

The constitution was not a long or complete document, but it laid the foundations for twenty years of Serbia's governmental life. It divided power between the prince and the Council, but in reality the latter was superior. The Council was to consist of 17 members, one from each of the seventeen districts, chosen from among the leading men in their respective districts. Most important, they could not be removed except with the consent of the Porte. In short, the Council could defy the prince with impunity so long as it had the confidence of the Porte.

Moreover, the constitution of 1838 eliminated the National Skupština, which had been given considerable power by the constitution of 1835. The Council did not want the Skupština, which might interfere with its work. And the Porte did not desire an assembly because it was much easier to influence the Council than the Skupština. It has been said that the constitution of 1838 divided power between the prince and the Council in such a manner that the Porte could influence the outcome of any matter by siding with one or the other party. Miloš realized that he was shorn of any significant powers, and declared that he could not rule in conjunction with seventeen councilors who would be the organs of the Sultan. Among other things, the prince had to choose his ministers from the Council, and if he dismissed them or they resigned, they went back to the Council. Not only were Council members irremovable, but in addition, new appointments to the Council could be made only upon recommendation by the Council itself. In this way, the Council became a self-perpetuating oligarchy. When Miloš suggested changes in the constitution, the members of the Council were opposed, styling themselves as *Ustavobranitelji* (Defenders of the Constitution)—that is, defenders of the constitution of 1838.

Miloš fled Serbia in April 1839, but he was back the same month, in part because of the urgings of the Russian Consul in Belgrade. He had some information that certain army units, which were hostile to the Council, were on the move toward Belgrade. Apparently, he thought this show of support unnecessary because he sought, unsuccessfully, to discourage them. Toma Vučić Perišić (usually known simply as Vučić), perhaps the most important leader of the Defenders of the Constitution and in modern times it would be said that he had "charisma," met these units with armed force and disarmed them. In this he had Miloš's support, but Vučić soon turned his newly-won power against Miloš and forced him to abdicate, which Miloš did in June 1839.

Following Miloš's abdication in 1839, his son Milan became prince, but he was on his deathbed and it is doubtful if he ever realized he was prince of Serbia. Thereupon the second son, Mihailo, became prince, but not for long. By 1842, the Defenders of the Constitution succeeded in driving the Obrenovićes from the throne, and in installing Alexander Karadjordjević, the son of Karadjordje, as prince of Serbia. This indicated a complete victory for the oligarchical Council, because for the present the Obrenovićes were out and the new prince owed everything to the Council, by whose constitution he was willing to be limited. Although styling themselves as Defenders of the Constitution, the members of the Council transgressed against it insofar as they overthrew a dynasty, which according to that same constitution had a hereditary right to the throne.

IV

Oligarchical Rule: 1838–1858

After the ouster of Prince Miloš, the oligarchy (Defenders of the Constitution) needed some three years to consolidate the regime, which stayed in power until 1858. Secure in their positions in the Council, they initially set up a regency for Miloš's minor son Mihailo, but subsequently forced him to resign from the throne, and chose Alexander Karadjordjević as the new prince of Serbia. This was the first example in modern Serbia of the use of the army for political purposes.

Defenders of the Constitution and Their Program

In order to justify and popularize their actions against Mihailo, the leaders of the oligarchy told the people that they were not rebelling against the prince, but only defending the constitution from him. Perhaps the most articulate of them (Vučić), a real demagogue, told the people that they were all equal, that they did not need to stand up for anyone or take off their hats in front of anyone. "All of us," he said, "have a right to hold our heads high, and none of us need to stand in the shade, because all of have a right to be warmed by the sun."

By concentrating on the unpopular actions of Miloš and Mihailo, the Council won considerable popularity. But its leaders did not have political or reforming ideas, and neither did Prince Alexander. This was not true of the intellectuals who were in the civil service, mainly Serbs from Austria who had come to Serbia after its qualified liberation from the Turks. Their main ideas were to establish personal security for the citizens, and to limit the prince. These ideas were to be realized through the creation of courts, a bureaucracy, and institutions (written laws and schools) that would tie them together.

This was the beginning of a detailed administrative organization of Serbia's governmental system. Personal rights, although not political, were secured. The prince was limited by an oligarchic center. By comparison with the past, these were relative gains. The very existence of the collegial Council protected the people against personal absolutism. In short, the first steps were being taken towards rudimentary modernization of the Serbian nation.

Credit must be given to the Defenders of the Constitution in that they perceived, in somewhat primitive and difficult circumstances, the need for some form of modernization. They did not really like the Serbs from Austria, but they saw the need to organize the judiciary and the civil service, and to establish an educational system that would provide the personnel for both. In these undertakings, they achieved considerable success. But in the realm of the economy they left much to be desired.

First Steps Toward Modernization

One of the first steps taken by the new regime was the promulgation of a Civil Code in 1844, which in the main followed the Austrian system. For the first time, a hierarchy of courts was established and the judicial power was separated from the prince. The most difficult problem was that of unqualified judges. Generally, they were illiterate, let alone holding law degrees. Even by the end of the regime in 1858, the number of really qualified judges was not more than about one-fourth of the total.

The situation with lawyers was even worse. In fact, most of the law work was done by individual civil servants when their regular duties permitted. These were in the main court secretaries and clerks. This practice was forbidden in 1843, and subsequently a type of lawyer did develop, mainly from among men who had failed at other things.

Despite the efforts of the Council to create a suitable judiciary, there were constant complaints concerning the courts, the most frequent being the slowness of their actions. The Defenders of the Constitution wanted to have courts as good as any in the modern nations. But the slowness led people to see only their shortcomings, and they could not appreciate the growing formalism of the courts. Yet this was the first attempt to get modern European courts in place of the patriarchal ones.

The problems of the civil service were similar to those of the judiciary. Legally, there were no set tasks, no hierarchy, and no set pay scales. The Council established classes and pay scales, and bureaucrats could not be dismissed without cause. In addition, they got titles and uniforms, and they were required to be clean shaven. And they were forbidden from engaging in trades and other private pursuits.

Under these improved conditions, many men sought careers in public service. But there were negatives as well. While civil servants could not be easily dismissed, they could be transferred, which often resembled exile. On the other hand, bureaucrats had great authority, particularly since criticism of the government was not permitted. By and large, however, the people accepted the notion that they should obey the bureaucracy.

Nevertheless, complaints piled up. The civil servants were not much better educated than the subjects. And since most of them migrated from Austria, they were increasingly looked upon as foreigners. Moreover, the power of the police to impose certain penalties was resented, particularly when they dismissed known or suspected Obrenović partisans in the civil service. In addition, toward the end of the Council regime, the bureaucrats were brought into the conflict between the prince and the Council, both sides seeking allies among them.

The Constitutional Defenders did create a legally secure position for the bureaucracy, and while improving the quality of the civil service, they did little to develop its professional competence. They did increase the number of schools, the aim being to create a higher quality of employees in the civil service and the courts. The first law courses were established in 1841, and the National Library was created in 1853.

Initially, the local communities built schools and paid the teachers. By the 1830s, there were 60 grammar schools with 69 teachers, the majority from Austria. In the 1850s, the teachers were selected and paid by the ministry of education. This was made possible in part by the enactment of a special school tax in 1855, the proceeds of which went into a special school fund. But the conditions for the teachers were not good. Pay was low and irregular, and the teachers were not held in high esteem by the people. A ministry of education was created in 1862 and primary schooling was made compulsory in 1863.

In 1839, for the first time, Serbian students in modest numbers were sent to study abroad, some to Austria and Germany, but increasingly to France. By 1858, some two hundred men had been educated abroad. Although a modest number, these men were to constitute the beginning of a native intelligentsia. They brought new ideas and elements of European culture.

A number of changes took place earlier. Austria had introduced a postal service in 1843, and Belgrade was connected with Europe by telegraph in 1855. A water supply was introduced in the 1860s, but a sewage system was not built until 1905. And Belgrade obtained an electrical plant in 1891, and by 1894 got electrically powered streetcars.

The first sign of dissatisfaction with the Constitutional Defenders' regime appeared among educated men, among students and professors. There were instances where the minister had or had not finished elementary school, whereas his secretary had a Paris doctorate. These younger men began to speak openly and critically. They recognized the need of institutions that would represent and defend the people's rights. Parliament was such an institution, but the Serbian Skupština did not exist during the Council regime. It met only once (1848) in a period of twenty years.

At the time that the Council oligarchy came to power, Serbia was economically backward in every way. Agricultural techniques were medieval. There were few roads, little money, and no economic organization on a national scale. Unfortunately, the oligarchy did little about Serbia's backwardness.

Improvement in living conditions was slow. Log cabins and mud huts from the Ottoman period were gradually replaced with homes made of solid materials. Brick and tiles, however, came only toward the end of the century. European-style architecture was introduced by 1850, mainly by architects from Austria and Hungary.

Some efforts were made to promote capital formation, including the creation of a national bank. But financial loans continued to be difficult to get, and interest rates remained high. Gains in agriculture, mining, and forestry were minimal or worse.

A well-known Serbian historian has said that in administratively despotic countries, more than anywhere else, the government is duty-bound to improve the welfare of the people. But the Defenders of the Constitution were technically and financially unprepared. These failures tended to make the people forget what the regime had done in the bureaucratic, judicial, and educational fields.

There were few if any organized and politically active interest groups at that time. The Western-educated elite helped to turn Serbia's economy toward Western Europe following the Paris Peace Conference (1856), at which the Great Powers assumed the role of Serbia's protectors, a role that Russia had played until that time, although in a somewhat ill-defined manner. But the Crimean War reduced Russia's ability to play the role it once played.

In the field of public finance, the country was faced with chronic deficits. This was contrary to Miloš's time when the national treasury had surpluses. The Council regime's initial popularity was due in part to its promise of low taxes. And it did not dare to raise taxes to pay for its various programs. Only with the Budget Law of 1858 was there a serious effort to bring some sort of order in public finance. By far the most important tax was a type of head tax. Late in its rule, the regime did raise taxes on exports, court costs, and forest cutting, but the income from these activities was not significant.

Developing Crisis in the Regime

In theory, under the constitution of 1838, supreme authority was shared by the prince and the Council. The latter, consisting of 17 members, was chosen by the prince from among the best known and most respected men among the people. But the law on the organization of the Council (1839) made it impossible for the prince to choose anyone who was not recommended by the Council. And once appointed, they could not be removed. The Council began as a group of eminent and popular leaders from their respective districts, for the most part men of relative wealth, but in twenty years the members of this self-perpetuating oligarchy were little known outside the capital.

Legislative power was vested in the Council. The prince could only recommend that the Council appoint a commission to give advice. The prince had no decree power, although he could veto Council proposals. The Council had control over the budget, and had the power to oversee the work of ministers. And the prince was required to appoint his ministers from the Council. The ministers in effect became a committee of the Council.

The basic conflict between the prince and the Council involved control of the administration. This was first evident in the military field, because the prince wanted the army personally loyal to him. Moreover, he claimed that he needed agreement with the Council only in the field of legislation. Consequently, by the mid-1850s he asserted that he could appoint ministers from outside the Council without the Council's prior recommendation. The Council resented his actions but could do little. At different times, the Council and the prince appealed to the Porte, but the latter was inclined to let Serbian matters disentangle themselves.

The conflict between the prince and the Council was exacerbated by the fact that the prince was appointing his wife's relatives to high posts. Important men, among them friends of his, advised Alexander not to pursue such an unwise course, but he apparently was unable to resist the demands of his wife's family.

The conflict had entered its third year when in 1857 the government uncovered a plot to kill the prince. The aims and motives were not very clear, although some of the conspirators seemed to have feared that the prince might strike first. The conspirators were found guilty and sentenced to death, but because of the Porte's intervention, Alexander commuted the sentences to life-imprisonment in chains.

Several other Council members were threatened with arrest unless they resigned. Six did so and their applications for pensions were approved. This was before the conspirators were tried and sentenced. Four other members were soon forced out, with the result that the Council was made up of men loyal to Alexander. Before long, however, a "loyal opposition" developed in the Council, not so much against the prince as against his ministers.

A more important opposition formed outside the Council. It consisted of former Council members who argued that their being forced out of the Council was in fact a coup on the part of the prince and therefore contrary to the Constitution of 1838. They appealed to the Porte and to the Great Powers who were the guarantors of Serbia's independence. For somewhat different reasons, the Porte and France and Russia forced Alexander to compromise, which favored the Council. The degrading "compromise" was accepted by Alexander because he had lived in fear of being deposed and the "compromise" looked like a relative gain.

Under the terms of the compromise, the prince forgave the Council for its opposition, and the Council forgave the prince for his illegalities. The six that had been forced out were returned to the Council. A new law on the organization was promised, which would resolve all disputed questions. All of this really favored the Council. In the process, the prince lost whatever prestige he had enjoyed with the public. He seemed weak—he could not even keep in prison the men who had conspired to kill him. The Council, on the other hand, appeared strong.

The new law on the organization of the Council further weakened the prince. His one-time absolute veto became merely suspensory. The criminal responsibility of Council members was so hemmed in that prior approval of the Council was required before a member could be brought to court. The principle that ministers would be selected only from men that the Council proposed was strengthened anew. Moreover, the Council gained additional powers of control over ministers, including the power to reprimand them and thus possibly to force them to resign. This was a rudimentary attempt to establish political responsibility in Serbia. It should also be mentioned that the new law made it impossible even for distant relatives of the prince to serve as Council members. The new organization of the Council represented the pinnacle of Council power. It was the master of legislative as well as administrative power at that time.

One man who was to play a critical role in the struggle between the prince and Council was Ilija Garašanin. The son of a well-to-do merchant, he had a private education, but had also traveled widely in Europe. Originally a member of the Council, he developed into a good administrator, serving as Minister of the Interior for ten years (1843–1852), a longer uninterrupted service in that post than any other man in previous Serbian history. Because of his anti-Russian attitude, however, he was forced out as a result of Russian pressure. Because of his ability and loyalty to the prince, however, he was soon brought back as Minister of Foreign Affairs. One of his first acts was to dismiss Vučić as cabinet advisor. But Alexander and Garašanin soon came into conflict simply because the prince did not want to listen to advice from his ministers. He wanted them merely to carry out his orders.

Following a temporary interlude, Alexander again bowed to Russian pressure and dismissed Garašanin. Because he did not want to return to the Council, Garašanin was given a pension. After the Peace of Paris in 1856, however, Garašanin returned to the Council and again was made Minister of the Interior. In that role he was soon to play a key role in the downfall of the prince and the Council.

It should be pointed out, parenthetically, that Garašanin was a far-sighted leader whose service to the nation did not end with the over-throw of the oligarchy in 1858. He was a systematic man; he had a foreign and domestic policy program for Serbia. In foreign affairs his basic position was that Serbia should not ally itself with either Russia or Austria, but should turn toward the Western powers, first of all, France. Some referred to him as the link between the older politicians and the young liberals educated mainly in Paris.

In the final analysis, the conflict between the prince and the Council meant that the nation had two masters, neither of which would let the other govern. Just as one time a need was felt to divide too concentrated authority, in the 1850s a need was felt for some concentration of a too divided authority. As this need became greater, the fall of Alexander and the Constitutional Defenders became all the more inescapable.

Revolution of 1858

In 1858, the regime of the Defenders of the Constitution was over-thrown by the Skupština. The prince and the Council were removed in the most peaceful revolution in Serbian history. What follows is but the briefest of accounts of how that Skupština was called, what it did, and how it did it.

Two important leaders, Vučić and Garašanin, decided after the fail-ure of the conspiracy to kill Alexander that he must nevertheless some-how be removed. They concluded that the only way was to have the Skupština overthrow him. But calling the Skupština was not easy because there were no established means for doing so. And the prince was not in favor of doing so. Moreover, some of the members of the Council were not for convoking it because they feared that the Skupština would simply become the tool of the master demagogue Vučić.

Vučić had traveled around agitating for the calling of the Skupština. He had a set speech in which he criticized the bureaucracy and called for reduced taxes, asserting that only the Skupština could save the "wretched

people." Garašanin operated more cautiously, working through Obrenović followers and the young liberal intellectuals. The former had been
badly persecuted but gained considerable courage as Alexander's repu-
tation and prestige fell. The young liberal intellectuals did not particularly respect the prince or the Council. But the idea of the Skupština
appealed to them because of its similarity to parliaments in Western
Europe with which they had become familiar.

When the ground had been prepared, Garašanin, without consulting
the prince in advance, raised the question in the Council of calling the
Skupština, asserting that in no other way could order be secured in the
nation. He met some opposition in the Council but subsequently got its
approval and that of the prince. The latter was reluctant but did not know
what to do if Garašanin should resign. Moreover, he thought that loyal
persons could be selected as members of the Skupština.

Under the law calling for the Skupština, there were two classes of
representatives: those chosen by the people and those selected by virtue
of their positions in the government. Of the deputies in the latter cate-
gory were 63 and the former 376. Because neither Alexander's partisans
nor Garašanin wanted Vučić in the Skupština, the law provided that
Council members and certain other officials would not be eligible for
election. In addition, the law specified that the president and vice-
president of the Skupština must be chosen from among its members.

Once the deputies had been chosen, it was fairly obvious that most
of them, may Obrenović supporters, were hostile to Alexander Karadjordjević. The prince and his group still had that solace which had been
the undoing of many regimes: "They would not dare!" More than that,
they did not think that Vučić and Garašanin would join the Obrenović
crowd. Finally, the prince was confident that as a last resort the army
would defend him.

Moreover, there was not agreement among the anti-Alexander
forces as to what or who should be put in his place. Certainly, the Vučić-
Garašanin contingent did not want Miloš's return. The liberals, for their
part, were willing to support the return of the Obrenović dynasty provided they could secure the establishment of a powerful parliament.

Certain liberal leaders became the main tacticians in the situation.
Their plan may be summarized under four points: (1) the initiative for

the overthrow of Alexander would be left to Garašanin and his well-to-do cohorts; (2) before deposing the prince, the liberals would propose a new law that would endow the Skupština with considerable power and which would guarantee its meeting annually; (3) a soon as the prince would be overthrown, the liberals would propose that the powers of the prince would be entrusted temporarily to the Skupština, thus avoiding a Vučić-Garašanin regency; and (4) at the moment of Alexander's overthrow, the Skupština would proclaim Miloš Obrenović prince. The main liberal tactician was Jevrem Grujić, who was chosen as one of the two secretaries of the Skupština.

Grujić's role was enhanced by virtue of the fact that the liberals' proposals for a new law concerning the Skupština became the first order of business. Moreover, during the discussion of the project, which took several days, he was its presiding officer. The man who had been elected its president, Miša Anastasijević, did not attend its sessions until the day that the proposal to oust Alexander was to be raised.

The liberals' project for future Skupštinas was far too radical for many of the influential delegates. Garašanin and his crowd, for example, were opposed to it, but went along with it after the liberals agreed that once passed, the project should be submitted to the Council for approval. The law was passed on these terms, but the attitude of the Skupština, which was convoked to depose the prince, is depicted by a noted Serbian historian, Slobodan Jovanović, as follows: "If I can overthrow the prince, then I can do everything else; there are no limits to my power."

Having succeeded in getting the law on the Skupština passed, the liberals left the initiative for the overthrow of Alexander in the hands of others. The Skupština quickly reached a verdict that it should ask for the prince's resignation. This was put in a written document, which also enunciated the principle that Serbia was an elective monarchy. A delegation was sent to deliver the document to the prince, and a resignation form was sent for him to sign. He did not oblige, but asked for 24 hours to think it over. He thereupon called a meeting of the Council, most of whose members urged him to resign. Since he did not wish to do so, he fled to the fortress, i.e., to the headquarters of the Turkish paša for protection. Some Serbian historians insist that Garašanin furnished the coach and escort for the prince.

By this act, the prince left the command of the armed forces in the hands of the minister of the interior, Garašanin, who wanted the Council and the Skupština to agree on a provisional government. But the liberals and the Obrenović followers were impatient in this period of uncertainty, particularly in view of what the army might do. Without delay, they succeeded in having the Skupština declare Alexander ousted, elect Miloš as the new prince, declare that the regency power would be in the hands of the Skupština, and made Stevča Mihailović commandant of the armed forces and the police. All of this was proclaimed to the public outside even before the various acts had been properly signed.

The groundwork for these acts had been prepared the night before, when it was learned that Alexander had fled to the city fortress seeking Turkish protection. Moreover, armed mobs, made up mostly of Obrenović supporters, were mobilized so as to provide a kind of shield around the brewery building in which the Skupština was meeting. The barracks of the Belgrade garrison were menacingly close—right across the street.

The Skupština merely informed the Council of its actions. It did not seek its approval. Vučić, although not a member, was permitted to speak, but his call for nullifying Miloš's return fell on deaf ears. But getting Garašanin to give up control of the armed forces was a different matter. He and other leaders realized that getting the army involved would result in bloodshed, and they did not want that. Garašanin realized that he had lost control of events, but he was for peace and order. In the end he agreed to surrender control of the armed forces, knowing that his trusted men in the barracks would act only on his orders.

His surrender of control of the armed forces was made easy when the liberals assented to the formation of a provisional government in which he was a member. Just as he had asked the army to remain at peace, he asked the Skupština to stay within the boundaries of the law. More than anyone else, Garašanin deserves the credit for the avoidance of a military clash between the army and the Skupština.

There is agreement among Serbian scholars that the army could have resolved the matter in Alexander's favor. It did not do so because there was a realization on the part of key men that in the process bloodshed could not be avoided, and they were unwilling to have that happen.

Moreover, Garašanin was for peace and order and his men in the barracks would heed his orders.

With the fall of Alexander, the regime of the Constitutional Defenders also came to an end. A revolution, which they had prepared, turned
out to be as much a revolution against them as against the prince. Originally popular, the oligarchy over the years lost contact with the people.
And the people's representatives, in a highly charged atmosphere, once
again turned to the Obrenović dynasty.

This was really an end of an epoch, and the beginning of a new one
for Serbia, which was beginning to exercise its *de facto* independence.
More than that, Serbia was breaking away from one type of system and
shifting toward another with its European neighbors. Movement was to
prove slow, and along its path were many hurdles.

V
Enlightened Despotism: 1858–1868

The overthrow of the Council oligarchy and of Prince Alexander in 1858, and the return of the Obrenović dynasty, ushered in a period of nearly ten years of absolute monarchical rule. Prince Miloš, who had been forced to abdicate in 1838, came back to rule for less than two years, passing away in 1860. His son, Mihailo, who was forced to flee in 1842, succeeded him. Mihailo's reign of some eight years has been most often described as enlightened despotism. It was a period in which absolute rule was little challenged and generally accepted.

Miloš's Reign, 1859–1860

Upon his return in 1859, Miloš talked of governing as a constitutional monarch. During his first reign men lost their heads because of the word "constitution." But Miloš had not changed much since 1839. He openly told the Turkish representative in Belgrade that he would not respect the constitution of 1838, which had been forced on him, and which had limited his powers.

Miloš really wanted to abolish the Council, but when he concluded that this was impossible, he sought to make it innocuous. In the main he selected national elders from his first reign, ordinary and uneducated men. Because the prestige of the Skupština had risen and that of the Council had declined, the Council caused no real difficulties for either Miloš or Mihailo.

Miloš had no problem with his ministers either. They served at his pleasure and he changed them frequently. He expected them to carry out his orders without asking questions. And in some matter, the military for example, he did not even tell his ministers what he was doing. Jevrem Grujić, who was in effect the president of the council of ministers, began to act as head of a parliamentary government, giving Miloš advice. Grujić sought to explain ministerial responsibility to him, but that did not appeal to Miloš. "What am I," he asked Grujić, "if you take responsibility for me?" Under such circumstances, Grujić could not remain a minister for long.

41

Miloš wanted to cleanse the civil service. But one of the real contributions of the Constitutional Defenders was the organization of a more competent civil service, whose members could be removed only through court action. Consequently, Miloš had difficulties in his attempted purge of the civil service, but he managed to trample on many of their gains.

Miloš was less successful in his efforts to interfere with the judicial process. The courts had established such independence that Miloš could not force them to rule contrary to the law. He could only take satisfaction in cursing out judges whose rulings he did not like, and he accorded himself that satisfaction in full measure.

The Skupština was in some ways the most significant institution at that time, not because it was strong enough to limit Miloš—a power it did not have—but because he allowed it full freedom of speech. It was his way of being informed about the people's complaints and needs. Here the people spoke; in all other political institutions it was Miloš who spoke. Although he could not get rid of his opponents as he once could, Miloš was nevertheless able, through arrests, pressure, etc., to isolate or neutralize them so that they constituted no danger to the regime.

In order to bring some satisfaction to the peasant masses, Miloš issued a number of decrees, proclaiming the principle that the land belongs to him who works it. The peasants complained about the high interest on government loans. The liberals told Miloš to lower the rates. The conservatives insisted that the peasants' troubles stemmed from their lack of knowledge about how to work the land and from the fact that there were too many holidays and too much time spent in taverns.

Neither the liberals nor the conservatives gave Miloš what he wanted—a quick solution. He took some ideas from both. In addition, he decreed that the peasant owed what he swore in church he owed. Although popular, this measure created much confusion, in part because false oaths were not a rarity. One of the consequences was that creditors stopped making loans. This decree was abolished when Mihailo came to the throne.

In brief, Miloš followed a policy of concessions, of letting up, of opportunism. For a time he permitted the conservative forces to speak out in the official and semi-official press. Then he changed editors and permitted the liberals to answer back. Initially popular, Miloš's regime soon became unbearable for conservatives and liberals alike. It was despotism that was fickle and equivocating. The one-time hero, as death neared, changed from day to day and seemingly without a steady course or definite direction.

Mihailo's Reign, 1860–1869

Mihailo came to power with one major aim—war with Turkey. More ambitious than his father, he wanted to stir up all of the Balkan peoples to revolt, with Serbia leading the way, and ultimately playing a major role in the creation of a South Slavic state, similar to the role played by Piedmont in uniting the Italian states. To prepare for war, it was necessary to unite all Serbs in a patriotic zeal, which would require a concentration of authority in the hands of the ruler.

In domestic affairs, Mihailo wanted to strengthen legality and to improve the material welfare of the country. He was surprised by the backwardness of Serbia's agriculture, the low cultural level of the people, the poverty, and the primitive nature of life. He was convinced that only a strong ruler could achieve the ends he sought.

Understandably, he could not say anything openly about war with Turkey, but he did indicate the need for a national army. His other aims were stated openly in a proclamation when he came to power in 1860 and in his speech from the throne to the Skupština in 1861. With respect to legality, he said, "As long as Prince Mihailo is on the throne, everyone should know that law is the highest will in Serbia, to which everyone without distinction must submit."

Mihailo's Political Institutions

In order to realize his goals, Mihailo believed that he had to make peace among the domestic factions, and to change the Constitution of 1838, particularly since the aim of that basic law was to weaken the prince. Characteristic of his attitude toward government in Serbia was his assertion that he could count on his fingers all the men in Serbia "who have a European education. There are no more than ten or twelve of them. The institutions of a country are not created for the twelve most educated men in it. To grant parliamentarism only because then Milovan Janković and a few others could give parliamentary speeches would be frivolous." He felt that the people were not ripe for a representative system. In commenting on the address given to him by the Skupština, he said to one of his secretaries: "Did you notice how many crosses there were on the address which you handed me? As long as the members of the Skupština cannot even sign their names...your haste to proclaim great freedoms is in vain."

To change the Constitution of 1838 would require, theoretically, Turkish approval. But for all practical purposes, Turkish power was nonexistent in Serbia. The Great Powers advised Mihailo not to adopt a new constitution, but to promulgate certain laws of a constitutional nature. Consequently, several organic laws dealing with the Council, the Skupština, and the central administration were adopted. This collection of laws constituted Mihailo's political and administrative system.

The once all-powerful Council was transformed into a bureaucratic instrument of the prince. The laws concerning the organization of governmental authority gave the prince unlimited powers over his ministers and over the bureaucracy. Another law took away the tenure of civil servants, enabling the regime to appoint and dismiss at will. Late in Mihailo's rule another law tightened controls over local government.

The law on the Skupština disappointed those who in 1858 had sought to give it such great importance. Gone were the paragraphs about the sovereignty of the Skupština, ministerial responsibility, and freedom of the press. Also disappointing was the proviso that it would meet every three years. Moreover, its powers now were merely consultative. By and large, the regime did not experience any serious difficulties with the three Skupštinas that were held during Mihailo's reign. During the last one, however, about one-fourth of the deputies demanded that the Skupština be given legislative powers, that ministerial responsibility be instituted, and that a law on freedom of the press be adopted. These demands were largely cries in the wilderness.

Mihailo recognized the importance of the press, mainly as a way of educating the public. But aside from the semi-official press, he did not permit any other. Private effort to establish a political newspaper were impeded at every turn. The only exception was *Srbija*, which was granted permission to publish in 1867, with the provision that it stay away from domestic politics, a prohibition it managed to circumvent from time to time. Opponents of Mihailo's regime were editing critical newspapers abroad, some of which were smuggled into Serbia, so that at least the most educated men in Belgrade knew what was being written.

Mihailo's Regime in Action

Mihailo was aware that the dynastic question was the principal cause of domestic discord and he sought to end it. He was forgiving and he sought forgiveness. He permitted Karadjordjević partisans, who fled or were forced to leave Serbia, to return. Those who had unlawfully lost their pensions had them restored or they were returned to government service.

For his ministers, Mihailo wanted to select leading men from different parties, but he discovered that uniting factions was impossible, so in 1861 he turned to conservatives. He appointed Ilija Garašanin prime minister, who stayed in power until 1867.

In the judicial realm, Mihailo began his regime with emphasis on the rule of law, yet in 1864 he found himself jailing five judges of the Supreme Court. They were found guilty, by a specially constituted court, of intentionally distorting the law and judging wrongly. They were sentenced to three years imprisonment, but were pardoned in something over a year. In the winter of 1863, the police had allegedly uncovered a conspiracy to overthrow the dynasty. Some 30 to 40 persons were arrested and tried. A number were found guilty and sentenced to prison terms of up to two years. When the matter came to the Supreme Court every one was set free, on the grounds that all that had transpired were confidential political discussions, but there was no proof of attempted preparations for action.

This ruling so alarmed the regime that it determined to take immediate action. It set up a special court, consisting of four members of the Council of State and three members of the Supreme Court, thus a majority of non-judges. This court based its decision of guilt on the findings of a three-man commission, and did not hear any of the accused judges. This wrecking of the Supreme Court hurt Mihailo and his government. It characterized the regime as indisputably despotic.

Mihailo's greatest achievement, in the opinion of most scholars, was his creation of a national army. The existence of a national army had a great impression on the people. National morale was high among peasants and intellectuals alike. Moreover, the considerable prestige which Serbia build up among the foreign powers was due in large measure to her military efforts. Mainly because of the army, Mihailo was successful in 1867 in forcing the Turks to remove their garrisons from Serbian cities—and without bloodshed.

But many people in Serbia were impatient for war with Turkey as a way of uniting Serbian lands which were still under Turkish rule. Mihailo spend a good deal of time in making alliances with other Balkan peoples, in the expectation that all of them would one day join in a common cause. Mihailo's chief helper was his premier and foreign minister, Garašanin. He was the first Serbian politician who realistically comprehended Serbia's diplomatic problems. In brief, he was distrustful of Russia and Austria, because help from either might easily lead to infringement of Serbian sovereignty. Therefore, he concluded, Serbia must look west, mainly to France.

Because of Mihailo's marital difficulties, Garašanin left the cabinet in 1867. For some time people had been asking why war with Turkey was being postponed. Mihailo's new advisors created additional doubts. Moreover, French support for the Serbian cause weakened because of France's concern with Prussia. France needed Austrian support and was not therefore inclined to alienate her by actively helping Serbia. In brief, war with Turkey was at best being postponed.

On the economic front, Mihailo's regime experienced meager gains. Several great economic reforms were projected, but little came of them. Plans with respect to railroads, river navigation, and the national bank never got beyond the investigation and planning stages. Some success was achieved in mining and the development of silk worms. The failure of the regime to do very much in the area of economic development was made worse by the fact that there were several bad agricultural years during Mihailo's reign. Even so, he contributed large sums from his personal fortune, in loans and grants, to meet certain governmental expenditures. Some defenders of his regime placed great emphasis on the need to liberate subjugated Serbs first, defending the postponement of economic problems for a later day.

Mihailo's Marital Problems and Crisis in Government

Mihailo's marital difficulties in the last three years of his reign led to acute differences among his ministers. His wife, Julia, was of Hungarian ancestry and a Roman Catholic. She was not popular in Belgrade, where her going to the Catholic church, especially when escorted by Mihailo, was regarded by the common people as shameful. The fact that she did not have children was thought to be most unfortunate. The Liberals regarded the marriage as a political mistake.

In early 1862 a love letter which Julia had written to Karl Arenburg came into Mihailo's hands. Among other things, the letter spoke of her separation from Mihailo and of her life with Arenburg in Venice. Mihailo decided that the marriage must end, but the Turkish bombardment of Belgrade that summer seemed to bring them together again. Early in 1863, Mihailo sent her on a political mission to London. While abroad she got together with Arenburg, and wrote to Mihailo suggesting a divorce. But he did not agree. In November 1864, she came back to Belgrade after an absence of nearly two years. In June 1865, Mihailo suggested divorce, but this time she refused. Finally, she left Serbia and did not return during his lifetime.

Toward the end of 1865, Mihailo and Julia reached an agreement to end the marriage in such a way that no mention would be made of the love letter to Arenburg. Moreover, Julia obtained a generous property settlement. As a Catholic, she could not get a divorce, but this might not have caused a serious problem had it not been for Mihailo's desire to marry again. Even this might have been tolerated except for the fact that the girl Mihailo wanted to marry, Katarina Konstantinović, was his second cousin. In 1865 he was a man of 40 and she a young girl of only sixteen.

The result was a serious rift among Mihailo's ministers. In the patriarchal Serbia of that day, his divorce was looked upon as a scandal. His proposed marriage to his second cousin was regarded as worse than a scandal; it was incest and forbidden by the canons of the Serbian Orthodox faith. His ministers were willing to treat the divorce as a personal matter, but not the proposed marriage. The principal spokesman was the prime minister, Garašanin. When he failed to persuade the prince, he had to go. Mihailo dismissed him in 1867.

Some ministers were willing to accommodate Mihailo. He had consulted with a close confidant, a Dr. Pacek, who after careful study of church laws prepared a memorandum which concluded that marriage between second cousins was permissible. Eventually, this memorandum was sent to the head of the Serbian church, but first a new ministry had to be formed. This task was entrusted to Jovan Ristić, who long served as Serbia's minister to Constantinople. Ristić proposed that all ministers be replaced except for the minister of war, Milivoje Blaznavac, who was for the marriage in any case. Ristić's plan was that given the ministers' approval of the marriage, Mihailo would agree to a liberalization of the regime. Mihailo viewed this as blackmail and dismissed Ristić.

Although basically a middle-of-the-road, conservative, Ristić, by virtue of his stand, became a hero of the liberals. Although another minister was chosen by the prince, Ristić seemed to be back in Mihailo's good graces within a short time. There were even signs that Mihailo, before he met his death on May 29 (Julian Calendar), 1868, was moving towards Ristić's view concerning the need for political reforms. He seems to have realized that the supporters of his despotic regime were opposed to his marriage, while those who would tolerate it were insistent on reforms.

The End of Mihailo's Reign

The plot to kill Mihailo and take over the government was well prepared. It was the work of a few individuals, most of whom suffered from personal disappointments or held grudges against Mihailo's regime. It was not the work of a political faction; the plotters simply believed that they would usher in a new regime which would not condemn them for getting rid of a despotic ruler. They succeeded in killing Mihailo, but the failure of the killers to pass on the news soon enough to their co-conspirators enabled his ministers to learn of the assassination first and to take the necessary steps to prevent the seizure of power.

Mihailo had taken an evening walk in the forest next to Topčider Park, which is some distance from the center of the city. He had done this many times before and usually without any guard. He had received anonymous letters urging him to be careful, but he was not concerned. As a matter of fact, he had forbidden a secret service guard, not wishing to give the impression that he was afraid. On the fateful evening, Mihailo was in the company of his love, Katarina, and her mother and grandmother. Of the two men who were along, only one was armed. The four assassins killed Katarina's mother along with Mihailo, and wounded the other members of the party, except the grandmother, who was first out with the news.

Ilija Garašanin was in Topčider Park at the time and was one of the first to hear the sad news. Although no longer a minister, he hurried into Belgrade and called the ministerial council together and began giving orders. A temporary regency was established that same night and four actions taken: (1) a proclamation that a Skupština would be called to decide on a new monarch; (2) a decree putting the army on emergency status; (3) creation of summary courts to try the guilty; and (4) calling an election of a Large National Skupština for the purpose of choosing a prince.

The next day, however, the minister of war, Blaznavac, decided the question of the prince in favor of Milan Obrenović, Mihailo's grand-nephew. Blaznavac ordered the army to swear allegiance to Milan, then a boy of 14, living in Paris. In this way, Blaznavac confronted the temporary regency with a fait accompli, a military coup, which they (and subsequently the Large National Skupština) could only ratify. A new regency was selected, consisting of Blaznavac, Jovan Ristić, and Jovan Gavrilović, none of whom was a member of the temporary regency. Moreover, no one of them was a recognized representative of past regimes, although Ristić had played important roles.

According to Serbia's eminent history professor, Slobodan Jovano-vić, "Blaznavac was the first to successfully utilize the army for the so-lution of domestic political questions, and his example was contagious. The history of Milan's son Alexander has beginning and ending chapters in an officers' conspiracy.... The Topčider catastrophe...announced the entry of the army into our internal politics."[1]

It is difficult to draw up a balance sheet on Mihailo's reign. Cer-tainly, he is one of the most prominent of Serbia's rulers. He had vision, and his horizons were not narrow. There is some question, however, as to his ability and that of his ministers to pursue their goals. In the light of the conditions prevailing in Serbia at that time, Mihailo achieved much, although he was no doubt a frustrated man. He gave unstintingly of him-self and his personal fortune. Unlike his father, who mixed with the people and whose residence was as open as any government office, Mihailo was reserved and more formal. He introduced pomp and cere-mony at his court, and audiences had to be arranged in advance. For the most part, he worked long hours, and associated almost exclusively with a narrow circle made up of his family and his ministers.

In the words of Slobodan Jovanović, Mihailo "was just, honest, noble; he had a high awareness of duty, much principle and steadfast-ness...patriotism...idealism.... But he lacked a certain intellectual

---

[1] *Druga vlada Miloša i Mihaila, 1858–1868* (Second Reign of Miloš and Mihailo), Belgrade, 1923, p. 277.

capacity that was required and he was indecisive"[2] It should be noted that Serbia of the 1860s was experiencing a time of political awakening, political parties were forming, and the people were beginning to demand a voice in public affairs. Whatever Mihailo's merits, it was clear that change was in the wind and could not long be postponed.

---

[2] *Ibid.*, pp. 151-152.

VI

Toward Parliamentary Government

The decade following the assassination of Prince Mihailo in 1868 witnessed several developments that were critical for the future of Serbian politics. The most important of these were: (1) the coming to the throne of a 14-year-old monarch in whose name a regency ruled until he legally became of age on his 18th birthday; (2) the making of a full-fledged Serbian constitution by that regency; (3) the explicit recognition in practice of the principle of ministerial responsibility; (4) the conduct of two wars with Turkey; and (5) the founding and organization of political parties. All of these elements played a role in the shaping of the beginnings of constitutional government in a decade of considerable uncertainty for Serbia.

The Monarch and the Regency

Because Mihailo had no direct heirs, his principal cabinet officers formed a temporary regency immediately following the assassination and called for the election of a constituent assembly to select a new monarch. The minister of war, Milivoje Blaznavac, was not satisfied with this arrangement, and quickly proclaimed Milan Obrenović, Mihailo's 14-year-old nephew then living in Paris, as the new prince of Serbia, and got the Belgrade garrison to swear allegiance to him. Blaznavac, who held the highest rank (colonel) in the Serbian army, had been in Paris at the time of the coup by Louis Napoleon and had become impressed with the power of bayonets in the hands of one daring enough to use them. When the Large National Skupština met, it recognized what had been done, and selected Blaznavac as first regent.

The political moving-force in the three-man regency was Jovan Ristić, who had been, as noted above, Serbia's representative in Constantinople from 1861 to 1867, and in the latter year was made minister of foreign affairs. Unlike most Serbian politicians who up to that time were sons of civil servants, merchants, or well-to-do peasants, Ristić

51

came from impoverished parents. As a bright young man, he studied in Germany with the aid of a government stipend, receiving a Ph.D. from Heidelberg University. Subsequently, he spent two years at the Sorbonne in Paris. He came away concluding that a regime which is too unpopular could not survive. Consequently, he told Mihailo that political reforms were necessary, which resulted in his dismissal. This brought him popularity among the young liberals, and in the years following the reign of the regency he became the leader of the newly-formed Liberal party.

Ristić became a regent at age 38, in part because he was a personal friend of Blaznavac. Although cool and arrogant, he was respected, and generally viewed as a superb statesman. As a moderate, he sought to combine a popular dynasty with the notion of political freedom, so dear to the Liberals. It is in this context that he played a key role in the drafting and adoption of the Constitution of 1869.

In the early years of the regency, the young monarch did not present a problem, but he was learning fast. He developed a dislike for Blaznavac and Ristić because some friends of his and advisers told him that the 1869 constitution reduced his power. Despite this, upon reaching age 18, he appointed Blaznavac prime minister and Ristić foreign minister. In addition, he made Blaznavac a general, the first one in Serbia. Ristić and Blaznavac might have clashed except for the fact that the latter died unexpectedly in March 1873, just as his star seemed to be rising.

By the time that Milan was 19, he had well-formulated ideas about politics in Serbia. He saw the peasantry as incapable of governing; the civil service as demoralized; and no upper class, which with the prince would be carriers of the state idea. He noted that there was no bourgeoisie and no independent intelligentsia. He grasped the essence of political questions quickly, but he no doubt erred when he thought of himself as smarter than all of his ministers. A cynic at a young age, he did not believe in God, and looked upon all men as bad. For him all of life was a struggle in which the more clever and the more merciless won out.

In addition, Milan early developed the habit of financial extravagance, which was to plague him during his lifetime. Moreover, he liked women and did not attempt to hide his doings. Before reaching his twenty-first birthday, he became engaged to Natalie Keško, whose father was Russian and whose mother (like Milan's) was Romanian. With his marriage only a few months old, his marital troubles were just beginning.

The Constitution of 1869

The Large National Skupština, which ratified the choice of Milan as prince and the three regents, directed the regency to bring about certain political changes. The major ones were: increase in the powers of the regular Skupština, freedom of the press, jury trials, and ministerial responsibility. In December 1868, a committee of experts produced a draft which was later ratified in June 1869 by an assembly of over 500 men.

When the constitution was being drafted, the regency informed and consulted with Austria-Hungary and Russia. The former was in favor and the latter against, but the Serbs assured the Russians that the reforms would be moderate. Turkey was not even informed, but the Turks accepted the new constitution without protest.

Perhaps the most significant aspect of the constitution was the elevation of the National Skupština to the position of a real legislative body. It stated that the "legislative power is exercised by the National Skupština with the prince." Then it provided that "no law can be promulgated, repealed, amended or reinterpreted without the agreement of the National Skupština." In case of great internal or external dangers, decree powers could be exercised, but these actions would have to be ratified at a later date by the Skupština. In actual law-making, bills could emanate from the legislative or the executive branch, but the constitution gave cabinet measures priority. The Skupština was given control over finance, although it could not attach unrelated matters to finance bills, and in case of disagreement, the existing budget could be extended by the monarch for one year if such an order carried the countersignature of all the ministers.

Aside from acquiring legislative power, the Skupština became a fixed institution with regular annual meetings; there was also a provision for special sessions. Three-fourths of its members were to be elected, with suffrage extended to males who paid a certain minimum in taxes. This came close to being universal male suffrage. The remaining one-fourth of the deputies would be appointed by the prince, although he was not obliged to appoint his full quota. The need for the appointed deputies stemmed from the fact that the draft of the constitution made civil servants ineligible for election, to which the constituent assembly added lawyers. The only way that eminent men of scholarship or experience in public affairs could enter the Skupština, therefore, was by appointment. Moreover, the constitution explicitly stated that deputies are not the representatives of those who chose them, but of the whole people.

The prince's contacts with the Skupština, except on formal occasions, were to be carried out through his ministers. Ristić had concluded that there never would be domestic peace until political responsibility was transferred to the ministers. In his speech to the Large National Skupština, he said that the constitution had placed the prince above every struggle and he was non-responsible.

The constitution said very little concerning the precise relationship between the prince and his ministers. It stated that the ministers were chosen and dismissed by the prince, and that they were responsible to him and to the National Skupština. Every act of the prince in state affairs had to be countersigned by the respective minister.

This suggests that ministerial responsibility was provided for, but other provisions of the constitution suggest that the framers were thinking in terms of legal rather than political responsibility. Ministers could not be members of the Skupština, but they could participate in parliamentary discussions and had the last word after other debate had ended. While there was no explicit provision for the resignation of ministers should they lose the confidence of the Skupština, the constitution did declare that ministers could be questioned and that they were obliged to furnish information. Moreover, there was a proviso that ministers could withdraw a measure anytime prior to the final vote, perhaps in recognition of the importance of parliamentary views.

As a compromise document, the constitution left many persons dissatisfied, especially those who thought that the Skupština's powers had been limited in several respects. The failure to be explicit about judicial independence, rights of local government, and guarantees about freedom of speech and press, all added to the dissatisfaction. Yet in view of Serbia's past history, the Constitution of 1869 was a great step toward constitutional government.

The Recognition of Ministerial Responsibility

The reign of the regency under the new constitution (1869–1872) was a period of relative tranquility and also one of fear. One man, Radivoje Milojković (Liberal), headed the cabinet during the entire period. With the aid and guidance of the regents, there was a systematic persecution of known Karadjordjević supporters. Fear was instilled in the populace with the execution of 17 men found guilty of being involved in the killing of Prince Mihailo. There was dissatisfaction, but there was fear of voicing it. The Skupština and the press did not go beyond the boundaries of moderation.

The government showed some concern with economic questions, but more emphasis was placed on education. A teachers college was established in 1873, and better salaries for teachers were instituted. A forestry school was founded in 1870. Students were warned, however, against involvement in politics. The budget was balanced largely because of special sources of income, and the first Serbian bank was created. The need to build railroads was recognized, but the necessary capital could not be found.

As indicated earlier, when Milan became of age in 1872, he first appointed Blaznavac and then Ristić as prime minister. Both were identified with the Liberals. The former died in 1873, and the latter, partly because he was unsuccessful in forming a cabinet with Conservative leaders, resigned after heading a cabinet of civil servants for six months. Although short-lived, Ristić's cabinet had the distinction of being the first in Serbia where the ministers were appointed on the recommendation of the prime minister.

Following Ristić's resignation, Milan appointed Jovan Marinović to head a cabinet of Conservatives, who a few years later took the name "Progressive." Within three months a number of laws were enacted, but Marinović is less well known for those laws than for the fact that he was the first Serbian prime minister to recognize explicitly that a cabinet could not stay in power if it did not have the confidence of the legislature. Under him ministerial responsibility became a fact of Serbian political life.

Marinović first posed the question of confidence to a somewhat bewildered special session of the Skupština in January 1874. Although he derived some satisfaction from the vote of confidence he won on this occasion, Marinović was aware of his cabinet's precarious position in a Skupština dominated by Liberals. Following the election of 1874, after a two-day debate on what should go into the address in answer to the speech from the throne, Marinović realized his minority position. In the actual vote, the cabinet's proposal won by a vote of 61 to 58, with three not voting. He interpreted this as an actual defeat, and the cabinet resigned. In this we have the first Serbian cabinet resigning as the result of an adverse vote in the Skupština.

The new cabinet that came into office in January 1875 experienced great difficulties and called for new elections in August, but resigned the day after the elections because the Liberals won a majority. Subsequent cabinets also resigned when they did not have the support of the majority of deputies. Jovan Ristić stated it best in November, 1879:

> I am not afraid of a lack of confidence. It could do nothing to my past, and it is not at all dishonorable to fall in parliament. In constitutional states, governments do not fall except in parliament. It is not good where it happens otherwise. I am confident that the minority will remain and that the majority will do justice to whom it belongs. For that reason, I propose that in the name of the government...that there be a roll call vote.

The roll call vote was favorable to the cabinet (113 to 25), with one abstention. But Ristić's opposition continued to be vocal, and he again had opportunities to lecture the deputies on the meaning of parliamentary government.

Serbian Politics and the Wars with Turkey

Following the defeat at the polls of the Stefanović ministry in August 1875, there was some turmoil before a new cabinet could be formed. The main question was whether Serbia should assist her compatriots in Bosnia-Hercegovina and thereby very likely get involved in a war with Turkey. The Liberals were the war party, but Milan and Conservatives were opposed. Milan did not think that Serbia could succeed, and the Great Powers advised noninvolvement. The press and public, however, were for war. After considerable difficulties and two acting or transitional cabinets, Milan became convinced that war could not be avoided. Thereupon in April 1876, he entrusted the formation of a new cabinet to the Liberals. Stevča Mihailović was made premier, and Jovan Ristić minister of foreign affairs. The coming to power of this ministry was in conformity with the secret actions of the Skupština of the previous September, when it voted in favor of helping the Bosnian rebels and approved the necessary loan to finance it.

As indicated above, war was declared in June 1876. Serbia's population was about 1.5 millions as opposed to Turkey's 40 million. Unofficially, the Serbian actions were supported by Russia. General Michael Cherniaev came with nearly 3,000 Russian volunteers, but the ill-prepared and inexperienced Serbian forces were being beaten when the Great Powers intervened. A shaky peace was concluded in February 1877, but the Serbs went again to war with Turkey in December, this time at the urgings of official Russia. The war ended in January 1878, with Turkey's defeat.

The end of the second war was bitterly disappointing. Although the Serbs fought side by side with the Russians, the latter signed the Peace of San Stefano with Turkey without Serbian participation. Moreover, the Russians treated the Serbs almost as an enemy, creating a Great Bulgaria at the expense of Serb-populated areas, some of which the Serbian forces had liberated. Because the Bulgarians had not participated in the war, the Serbs asked for an explanation. They were cynically told that Russian interests came first, then Bulgarian, and then Serbian. Although much of San Stefano was undone at the Congress of Berlin 1878, the Russians had added insult to injury by promising to Austria-Hungary the occupation of Bosnia-Hercegovina, and without telling the Serbs what they had done. It is understandable, therefore, that Milan, who in the first half of his reign was under Russian influence, should become Russia's sworn enemy in the second half.

In large measure because of his effective work at the Congress of Berlin, Jovan Ristić was made prime minister in September 1878. He immediately called for new elections, which the Liberals won. At the same time, a coherent opposition group of 40 deputies (out of 172) came into existence, forming the nucleus of what soon became the Radical party. At the second session of the Skupština in November 1879, the opposition candidate for the presidency of parliament received 71 votes. The position of the Ristić cabinet became shaky, partly because the opposition was more daring and partly because Ristić's popularity had declined, principally because of difficult post-war problems. In October 1880, the Ristić cabinet fell, not because of an adverse vote in the Skupština but because Ristić resigned when he could not go along with Milan in policies which would make Serbia economically dependent upon Austria-Hungary.

The Ristić cabinet had been the culmination of Liberal party rule. His fall was also the fall of the Liberal party as a ruling party. It was also the beginning of Milan's swimming in anti-parliamentary waters. Although Ristić was one of Serbia's greatest statesmen in the 19th century, he did not seek favor with the palace nor did he have an inclination to lead the masses. What he succeeded in doing in that critical decade can be attributed in large part to the fact that both the monarch and Serbian democracy were young, but that should not minimize Ristić's role.

Ristić's tutelage in that crucial time moved Serbia significantly toward constitutional government. Those entrusted with leading Serbian politics understood the spirit and limitations of the 1869 Constitution. By 1880, however, the leaders of the emerging Radical party were determined that the people's representatives in the Skupština should be dominant. At the same time, Prince Milan was convinced that the monarch's powers were eroding, a development that he increasingly resisted, leading to a serious confrontation. To better understand the political forces at work at that time, a brief description of the growth and formation of political parties in Serbia is in order to better understand political developments.

Political Parties

Political parties, as well-defined groups or movements, came into existence in Serbia only in the 1870s. Formal organization of parties with written programs began about 1880. Groups struggling for power (or seeking limits on the powers of others), however, were in evidence much earlier. They began with Serbia's first successful revolution in 1804. The early struggles under Karadjordje and Miloš cannot be defined clearly in class or ideological terms, although they left their mark in the form of specific political institutions. In the late 1830s, however, certain well-to-do merchants and high civil and military functionaries succeeded in limiting Miloš through the creation of a Council, which became stronger than Miloš and forced his abdication.

The leaders of the oligarchy that unseated Miloš were men who had held high military and bureaucratic posts. They employed democratic terms but they were not democrats. In addition to their demand for free trade, they also sought guarantees for private property and legal security, as well as prestige for the bureaucracy. It was the isolation of the oligarchy from the people and the abuses and indifference of its bureaucrats that brought the end of their regime in 1858.

As we look at the political groups and movements of the 1860s and 1870s that were to become the main political parties in Serbia, we also need to keep in mind that throughout the 19th century many Serbs found themselves the uncompromising adherents of one or the other dynasty— Obrenović or Karadjordjević. Some observers have pointed out that the struggles of the partisans of the two dynasties throughout the 19th century were in a sense akin to struggles between political parties.

The Liberal Party

During the rule of the oligarchy, educated men were respected, and the regime sent a modest number of promising young scholars to study in Western European universities. Upon their return, however, they soon became critics of the existing system. These liberal intellectuals, the nucleus of the future Liberal party, were first recognized as a political force when they combined with the Obrenović partisans in the 1858 Skupština that carried out a bloodless revolution against the Defenders of the Constitution and against Prince Alexander.

Unhappy with Prince Mihailo's rule, the liberals could do little. During a large part of that time, Jovan Ristić, Serbia's leading statesman at the time, was a broker between the prince and the Liberal leaders. Toward the end of Mihailo's regime, as Ristić began pressing Mihailo for liberal reforms, he attracted liberal support and in fact became the leader of what at best could be said to be a loosely organized Liberal party.

Perhaps more than anything else, the Liberal party demanded annual meetings of the Skupština. They insisted that it was the oldest, most significant, and most sacred Serbian political institution. In their arguments they even harked back to the ecclesiastical assemblies of medieval Serbia. They wanted the Skupština to have real legislative powers, and they believed that the ministers should be responsible to it. Moreover, the Liberals were uncompromising nationalists. Concern for their compatriots still under foreign rule was high on their political agenda, a concern that led them to two wars with Turkey. They hated all symbols of Turkish influence in Serbia—especially the ever-present fez—and worked to eradicate them.

During their rule in the 1870s, the Liberals did not have much in the way of organization. To a large extent the government bureaucracy served as the party's office staff. Only in 1880 did the party formulate an organizational statute, with local committees and the Main Committee. In 1881, the party published a formal program which emphasized preservation of political freedoms at home and unification with Serbia of Serbs still living under foreign rule.

The Progressive Party

The Progressive party sprang from a group of young conservatives, imbued with Western liberal ideas, whose basic program was "law, freedom, progress." They were joined by a few one-time Liberals, partly because the Progressives' social composition was akin to that of the Liberals. The party was led by a few leading intellectuals, but they never managed to put down roots among the masses.

The Progressives came into their own in 1880 and stayed in power for seven years. They had eclipsed the Liberals partly because of the high costs of the two wars with Turkey and partly because of the Liberals' inclination toward a tariff war with Austria-Hungary, which business interests did not want. But just as they got to power, the newly-founded Radical party captured the support of the peasantry.

The Progressives established a democratic organization structure with a card-carrying membership. In 1881 and after, they created local area committees, as well as annual congresses, but they did not pay much attention to agitation and propaganda. Moreover, they did not have the fiery orators found among the Radicals, nor did they attract a significant number of followers.

In power, however, the Progressives promulgated important reforms. If for the moment we put aside the fact that they became Milan's tool in putting down the Radical rebellion in 1883, we must recognize the measures they enacted. They were motivated by the desire to modernize and Europeanize Serbia, to transform a patriarchal country into a contemporary European state. Among the laws passed were those dealing with the freedom of speech and press, judicial independence, freedom of association and organization, free elections, compulsory education, and reforms in local government and taxation. In addition, they launched the building of railroads, and they established a national standing army.

Finally, the fate of the Progressives was closely tied to King Milan's fate. His problems were their problems. In the beginning they were a party of freethinking Western intelligentsia. The appearance of the Radical party, however, derailed them. In their eyes the "despotism of the masses" became a greater danger than the despotism of the monarch. Never having had strong roots among the people, they rapidly became a palace camarilla. When their patron abdicated in 1889, they ceased to be a significant force in the politics of Serbia.

The Radical Party

The ideological father of the Serbian National Radical party was the socialist Svetozar Marković, but he died in 1875 at the age of 27, before the party got organized. The budding movement fell under the influence of the more practical bent of his followers. Initially, two brilliant publicists (Adam Bogosavljević and Pera Todorović) took most of Marković's ideas to the peasant masses, but they were careful to avoid mentioning the socialist ideas that would have been repugnant to the peasants. They emphasized Marković's attacks on the bureaucracy and his call for organizing the nation politically on the principle of self-government. Moreover, they championed his call for guaranteeing all basic political rights, and his demand that the ministers be responsible to the Skupština.

The real founder of the Radical Party was Nikola Pašić, who determined its ideological and organizational cast, and who was to be its leader (with brief interruptions) until his death in 1926. He was first among the Radicals to be elected to the Skupština in 1878. In 1880 he organized the opposition deputies into a coherent caucus, the first to be formed in Serbia. In the latter year a party program was worked out and published in the newly founded party newspaper, *Samouprava* (Self-government), in January 1881. Moreover, party statutes were formulated and the first national congress held in 1882, at which Pašić was elected president without opposition. At that time he said that "states which reached the highest degree of enlightenment were those in which the people ruled," and therefore it was necessary to change the constitution "in the spirit of democratic freedoms, in the spirit of the people's sovereignty, in the spirit of self-government."

In general the Radicals could speak the language of the peasants. The following is a sample, almost word for word, of their ability to put things in ways easily understood by the masses:

> People without a constitution are like nomads who live on the bare ground under an outstretched canvas; people with a bad constitution are like men who live in small and miserable thatched huts which are full of smoke, darkness, cold, and dirt; people with a good constitution are like men who have large well-lighted rooms in which all live in warmth and comfort.

The ability to talk in these terms to largely illiterate peasants quickly secured the Radicals with a large and enthusiastic following.

The party's program, dealing almost exclusively with domestic affairs, stressed the need of amending the constitution so that the Skupština would be freely elected by all adult citizens, that it have full legislative power, and that it meet annually on a specified date. Moreover, the program demanded reforms in the bureaucracy, which would make administration simple, cheap, effective, and that it respect local self-government. In addition, the program called for a direct and progressive income tax, educational opportunities for all, and for economic improvements. In foreign affairs, the program stressed the need to liberate the still subjugated parts of Serbdom, to strive for closer relations with Montenegro and Bulgaria, and to strengthen the national army (up to that time a type of people's militia), leaving the standing army the principal task of training the national army. Before the constitution could be amended to achieve some of the above-mentioned objectives, the program demanded legislation guaranteeing freedom of speech and press, freedom of association, recognition of local self-government, and security for persons and property. Finally, the program created the party organ, *Samouprava*.

Under Pašić's guidance, the Radical party was the first political party in Serbia to organize systematically. Moreover, Pašić made it a highly disciplined party, with the rank-and-file expected to support the leadership. The most important policy-making body was the Main Committee, consisting of the main party leaders in Belgrade. When the Skupština was in session, however, the caucus of the party's deputies was more powerful.

Although the party statute provided for a dues-paying membership, success was instantaneous. The membership was made up mainly of peasants, with teachers and priests in the leadership positions, but the party soon began to attract vocal intellectuals—literary figures and pro- fessors. The party also became attractive to merchants who liked the idea that government should cost less. Moreover, the party experienced im- mediate success at the polls. These successes may also have contributed to the Timok rebellion in 1883, following which the party was severely repressed and many of its leaders shot or persecuted. But the people's loyalty and attachment to the party could not be destroyed.

The widespread and overwhelming successes of the Radicals also served to discourage the formation of minor parties. A few of Svetozar Marković's ideological followers, however, sought unsuccessfully to organize a socialist party in 1881, believing that the Radicals had aban- doned Marković's basic ideas. Ultimately, of course, a socialist party was bound to be organized. In 1903, under the leadership of Dimitrije Tucović and Radovan Dragović, the Serbian Socialist Democratic Party was formed. They did not attract many followers, and the Radicals con- tinued to be the main political party force in Serbia.

Political Mobilization and Elections

Communicating political ideas and mobilizing support for political programs or movements in any systematic way was not much in evidence in Serbia until the 1870s. To a degree it was done before that time by the prince, the Orthodox church leaders, and by the few educated men, but it was not systematized, and it was in the main in the form of oral communication. At the same time oral discussion should not be minimized because for decades, even after the printing of newspapers, a largely illiterate population was educated politically in that way. Serbian peasants seem to have had an extraordinary interest in and liking for politics. Even if they could not read or write, they listened to discussions, asked questions, and expressed themselves. With the expansion of formal education and the coming into existence of newspapers, it became possible for the expression of political opinions to be more widely shared and for political alternatives to be brought into sharper focus.

As the political parties developed, it became accepted practice that each party have at least one known organ, usually a newspaper. Some parties also published periodicals and political tracts. In the case of the Radicals, Svetozar Marković and his colleagues put out newspapers several years before the formal founding of the party. These were banned after publishing for a few months, partly because they had defended the Paris Commune. So long as the socialist press limited itself to economic questions, however, it was left alone. The initial press laws under the 1869 Constitution provided for a relatively free press, and many new newspapers came into being, although several failed for economic reasons. At times newspapers did not dare to print certain things, but at the same time they could complain that the press was not free. Moreover, there were times when the cabinet in power had no newspapers while the opposition had several. When the press laws were altered to make censorship and the banning of newspapers easier, several satirical publications came into existence, and they enjoyed considerable success. Press laws were changed several times in the latter decades of the 19th century, sometimes in favor of greater freedom and at others in the form of greater restrictions.

As time moved on, in addition to the partisan press, the number of publications about politics increased rapidly. Some of these were original studies and some were translations of Western European authors. For a long time, the content of Serbian publications was weighed heavily in terms of the needs of a freely elected Skupština, responsibility of ministers, security of political liberties, and issues of national independence. As these issues were in the process of being resolved, particularly after 1869, political party struggles tended to concentrate on the question of control of government jobs, foreign debt, foreign control of the salt monopoly, and subsequently the foreign ownership and operation of railroads, as well as Austria-Hungary's exploitation of the state.

With the establishment throughout the peasant areas of local party committees by the Radicals, political communication and mobilization took on a personal aspect. The people were told not only the party's ideas and programs, but were also informed of their electoral rights and what to do if these rights were infringed. In addition, visits by national leaders and the organization of political rallies made election campaigns more meaningful and more dramatic. Other parties sought to emulate the Radicals, but their successes were indeed limited by comparison.

Although there were no electoral laws prior to the adoption of the Constitution of 1869, the really significant ones for this study are those of 1870 and 1890. The 1870 law provided that electors had to be 21 years of age and that they pay some amount in direct taxes. Because the latter provision was somewhat vague and subject to varying interpretations, Serbia could be said to have approached universal male suffrage. Lists of eligible voters were posted in advance of elections, and appeals could be made by persons who believed themselves eligible. Voting was direct in the cities and indirect in the peasant areas, and it was public. To qualify as a candidate for the Skupština one had to have reached the age of 30 and to have paid a higher direct tax than was required of electors.

The 1890 electoral law followed from the Constitution of 1888. It provided that an elector need to pay 15 dinars in direct tax, but because members of cooperatives (*zadruga*) were assumed to have paid at least that much by virtue of tax payments by the cooperatives, this was another step toward universal male suffrage. As cooperative membership dwindled in subsequent years, however, a significant number of Serbs were disenfranchised by 1912. Secret voting, through the use of small rubber balls, was introduced by the electoral law of 1890. It also provided for direct election of deputies in the cities, with a runoff if no candidate received an absolute majority of the votes cast. In the peasant areas, several deputies were elected from a single electoral district, and these were apportioned to party lists on the basis of proportional representation. A specific date was set for elections, and provisions were made for special elections to fill vacancies as well as to dissolve the Skupština.

In order to be eligible as a candidate under the 1890 law, a person had to have reached the age of 30 and to have paid 30 dinars in direct taxes. Unlike the 1870 law, however, the 1890 statute made civil servants (except those in police administration) eligible, but if elected and seated, they would lose their positions in the bureaucracy. Soldiers and active officers could neither be candidates nor voters.

The electoral law, which followed the 1903 constitution, was closely patterned after that of 1890.

Some of Serbia's elections were free and others subject to a great deal of government pressure. Prior to the wide awakening of the people by the political parties (i.e., prior to 1880), the cabinet in power could pretty much get the results that it desired. The general tendency was toward freer elections, but there were setbacks. The elections of 1870 and 1874 were accompanied by a good deal of government pressure. Those in 1875, 1877, 1878 and 1880 were relatively free. The elections of 1883, the first with organized parties so that it was known to which party each candidate belonged, were the most free up to that time. But because the results were so unacceptable to King Milan and his close associates, the resulting Skupština was adjourned as soon as it met. In the elections of 1886 and 1887, there was considerable police pressure, but those in 1888 and 1889 were fully free.

The elections of 1897 were relatively free, and with the return in 1903 of the Constitution of 1888 and the electoral law of 1890, with minor modifications in both, Serbian elections again became fully free and remained so thereafter.

VII

Milan Obrenović vs. the Radical Party

Milan began the second half of his reign with a determination that he was not going to govern with the Liberals, mainly because their leader, Jovan Ristić, had not hesitated to disagree with the monarch. When Ristić resigned after one of their disagreements, Milan turned to the Progressive party, which was blessed with some gifted leaders who were initially referred to as "young conservatives." Unfortunately for Milan and for them, the Progressive party never won a significant popular following, primarily because just as they came to power the newly founded Radical party captured the fancy of the peasant masses. Nevertheless, Milan kept the Progressives in power for seven years despite the fact that their party was the smallest of the three. In the end, however, he not only gave way to the Radical majority, but also presided over the making of a truly democratic constitution, abdicated his throne in favor of his 13-year-old son, and brought back Jovan Ristić to be the principal regent—the same Ristić who had been regent during Milan's own minority twenty years earlier.

First Years of Progressive Party Rule

Milan entrusted the formation of the first Progressive cabinet to Milan S. Piročanac in October 1880. New elections brought mainly Progressives and a loose association of Radicals to the Skupština. The Radicals, because they were hostile to the Liberals, for a time cooperated with the new cabinet. This was especially true when the Progressives were enacting laws of freedom of speech and association. Milan was not too happy with these laws, but the Progressives were willing to follow his dictates, especially in foreign policy. They cooperated with Milan in ousting the head of the Serbian Orthodox Church, Metropolitan Mihailo, and in supporting Milan's secret treaty of June 1881 with Vienna, which in effect made Serbia an economic and political vassal of Austria-Hungary. The precise contents of the treaty were known only to two or three Progressive leaders.

Despite an auspicious beginning, the Progressives were soon in trouble. The ouster of Metropolitan Mihailo and several bishops was not popular. The large-scale changes in the civil service that benefited the Progressives were even more unpopular. Moreover, the Radicals soon formed their own parliamentary caucus and were ready to do battle when an appropriate opportunity arrived, which was not slow in coming. In January 1882 it became known that the *Societe de l'Union Generale*, with whom the Progressives had concluded a loan for the building of railroads, as well as agreements for the building of railroads, had gone bankrupt.

There was an understandable concern about the consequences of the bankruptcy for Serbia. The cabinet did not dare face the Skupština, and as a diversion, Serbia was proclaimed a kingdom and Milan king in February 1882. This sudden and unanticipated proclamation was apparently taken as a way of minimizing the impact on the public of the consequences of the bankruptcy. But the Progressives' parliamentary difficulties were not overcome thereby. It soon became common knowledge that the borrowed money was left with the *l'Union Generale* to draw interest with the consequences that Serbia's loss would more than exceed its total annual government budget.

In March 1882, after unsuccessful efforts to get at the truth through interpellations, 53 deputies (51 Radicals) resigned, leaving the Skupština without a quorum. They believed that their resignations would force new elections. But the Progressive leaders simply got the Skupština officers to accept the resignation and to call for special elections to fill only the vacated posts.

The Progressives hoped to elect at least 12 deputies in the special election which would ensure a quorum. King Milan, no longer even pretending to behave as a constitutional monarch, traveled throughout Serbia for a whole month, engaging in anti-Radical agitation. But success eluded him and the Progressives. The latter won five contests and the Radicals 45. Again the Radicals resigned, but Milan refused to accept their resignations.

Again new special elections were held to fill the vacant seats, but with the proviso that if the voters again voted for those who had resigned, these would not be counted. Instead, those receiving the next highest vote would be declared voted. In this way, some men entered the Skupština with no more than a handful of votes, some as low as two votes. Such deputies became known as "two votes." The Progressives got their quorum. Surprisingly, the Radicals won ten seats because no votes were cast for any opposing candidates. No one among the Progressives really believed in the legality of such elections. Consequently, Piročanac and his colleagues again tried to resign, but were prevailed upon to stay by King Milan and the Austrian minister. With the help of the "two votes," the cabinet enacted several measures aimed at the Radicals, such as limiting the freedom of the press and introducing a heavy monetary fine for absence from the Skupština aimed at denying a quorum. Some other important laws were enacted, providing for: (1) compulsory elementary school education, (2) the establishment of a standing army, (3) the setting up of a national bank, and (4) the creation of rules governing church authorities.

Piročanac stayed on because Milan could find no alternative. For a time Milan toyed with the idea of a "putsch," but got no support for it either inside or outside Serbia. What began as a struggle between the Progressives and the Radicals turned into a struggle between the king and the people. Prior to new elections that were to take place in 1883, further actions were taken against the Radicals, including the dismissal of their sympathizers in the civil service (including teachers) and the banning of the opposition press.

Radical Electoral Victories and the Timok Rebellion

The elections held in September 1883 were a disaster for Milan and the Progressives. The Radicals elected 61 deputies and the Progressives 34, with the Liberals getting 11 and 7 with no party affiliations. The cabinet resigned, but Milan, instead of turning to the Radicals, appointed a cabinet of bureaucrats headed by the arch-conservative Nikola Hristić. Neither he nor Milan wanted to have anything to do with the Radicals. The Skupština was opened with one decree and then adjourned with another, all in a matter of ten minutes. This slap in the face to the victors left everyone wondering what would happen next.

While both sides waited, a rebellion broke out in the Timok region of eastern Serbia where the Radicals were especially strong. The immediate cause was the government's collection of national militia firearms that had been left in the hands of the people. This action, which could not have come at a worse psychological moment, had been considered earlier when the Progressives created the standing army, but had not yet been implemented. The Radicals had been discussing what might happen, but the party leaders in Belgrade were surprised and unprepared when the rebellion occurred. After one or two hurried and clandestine meetings of the party's Main Committee, the party leader, Nikola Pašić, quietly crossed over into Austria-Hungary, avowedly going via Romania to join the rebellion. Before reaching Serbian territory, however, he got word that the rebellion had already been put down. For the next six years he lived in exile, mainly in Bulgaria.

The government's action against Radical leaders was swift and brutal. A state of emergency was proclaimed and the standing army was sent after the rebels. A summary court, established to try the offenders, sentenced 94 to death and over 600 to varying prison terms. Of the former, 20 were executed, among them Radical deputies, priests, and teachers. In addition, the members of the Radical Main Committee were tried, although evidence against them was lacking. Three of them were sentenced to death, including Pašić who was tried in absentia. The sentences of the other two were reduced to 10 years imprisonment.

After the suppression of the Radicals, the Skupština was dissolved and new elections held in January 1884. Except for some nondescript oppositionists, the whole Skupština was made up of government supporters. The veteran Nikola Hristić resigned, and Milan turned to Milutin Garašanin, soon to become leader of the Progressive party. His cabinet succeeded in getting enacted several laws that strengthened the position of the central government at the expense of local government and political freedom generally. In addition, several other measures were passed which were designed to put Serbia's finances in order. But Milan's troubles were not at an end.

Milan's Troubles

Milan might have been able to continue ruling with the Progressives had it not been for certain critical problems. The major ones were: (1) the disastrous war with Bulgaria in 1885, (2) his difficulties with his wife Natalie, and (3) the differences that developed between him and his ministers. These problems, in combination, constituted overwhelming difficulties for Milan, which can be treated here in the briefest form.

The war with Bulgaria was precipitated by Bulgaria's occupation of Eastern Rumelia in September 1885, which Milan viewed as a violation of the Treaty of Berlin (1878) which had prevented the creation of a Great Bulgaria. When his appeal to the Great Powers failed to produce any action, Milan declared war. Unprepared diplomatically, financially, or militarily, Serbia suffered defeat and consequently was forced to accept a peace imposed by the Great Powers. The outcome might have been different if Milan had explained his thinking to the people, if he had used the national militia as well as the standing army, if he had not dismissed most of the military commanders who led Serbia's forces against the Turks in 1876–1878, and if he had not held back certain forces which he wanted to have on hand in case of internal disorder.

The first consequence of the unsuccessful war was Milan's desire to abdicate, but the Progressive ministers dissuaded him in no uncertain terms. The realization that his estranged wife Natalie might assume the role of regent also deterred him. Moreover, Austria-Hungary wanted him to stay on the throne. But in that case, Milan realized that under the existing circumstances, if he stayed on the throne, he would somehow need to make peace with the Radicals. After an initial effort to promote a Progressive-Liberal agreement failed, Milan went to the Belgrade prison to seek the assistance of Pera Todorović, a member of the Radical Main Committee, who was then serving a ten-year sentence. While Todorović was willing, Milan's subsequent talks with other Radical leaders were to no avail. Consequently, Milan hoped for a Radical-Liberal combination, but the Progressives managed to stay on, but not for long, mainly because of the estrangement of Milan and Natalie.

Milan and Natalie had separated before the Serbo-Bulgarian war, in part because they were seemingly incompatible (Milan was not a faithful husband), and in part because she did not approve of Milan's pro-Austria policy and his desire to educate their son Alexander in Vienna. During the war she returned to Serbia and won considerable popularity through her concern for the wounded. Milan imagined that she wanted to drive him from the throne and that she wanted to become the regent. But it seems that she had given thought to the latter after Milan indicated he wanted to abdicate for the whole dynasty. In any event, a mutual hatred for each other grew rapidly. Milan informed her by letter that life together for them was no longer possible and that she would have to leave Serbia.

When informed of Milan's letter, Prime Minister Garašanin resigned, but was persuaded to withdraw his letter of resignation after an arrangement had been worked out for Natalie to live abroad. As a way of hiding their differences from the public, it was announced that Natalie would live abroad in connection with the education of their eleven-year-old son. Nevertheless, Milan no longer had confidence in Garašanin, and was already plotting to make a change when word reached him—a piece of inaccurate news it seems—that Natalie was returning to Belgrade. He ordered that she be prevented from doing so, by force if need be. The result was a stormy session with his prime minister, who resigned the next day.

After considering various options, Milan concluded that the only way out was abdication. But there were many uncertainties. He would need to appoint a regency which would rule during his son's minority. In that case, the most likely candidate for first regent was Jovan Ristić, whom he thoroughly disliked. Nevertheless, his first step was to appoint a Liberal-Radical ministry in June 1887, headed by Ristić. In the ensuing elections (September 1887), the Liberals won 59 seats and the Radicals 87. Milan concluded that it would be easier to work with one party rather than two. When his wishes became known, the coalition cabinet fell apart, and he turned to Colonel Sava Grujić, who identified with the Radicals, as prime minister. Within four months he resigned because of his apparent sympathy for Natalie.

Milan erred in identifying Grujić's views with the Radical party, which had not taken a stand on the divorce question. Consequently, he decided that he needed another cabinet to settle the divorce problem. Milan turned to the time-tested and dependable bureaucrat, Nikola Hristić, who put together a cabinet in April 1888. In the meantime, Milan was angered by a provocative letter from Natalie, and submitted a divorce petition to the head of the Serbian Orthodox Church and so informed Natalie, who was in Wiesbaden with their son Alexander. It soon dawned on Milan that she might take off with the precious hostage to Russia. He advised the German government of his worries. In a botched situation, the German police, on orders relayed from German Chancellor Bismarck, took Alexander away from Natalie. This act was characterized as scandalous and Milan got most of the blame both at home and abroad. Objectively speaking, Milan, Natalie and Bismarck were all at fault.

Prior to Bismarck's act, Milan had offered Natalie a settlement which in many respects was generous. He proposed to drop the divorce action, and to let her keep Alexander for five years, but she must stay away from Serbia. It was when she turned a deaf ear to these proposals that Milan took action that led to Bismarck's act. Then Milan turned to the Church authorities to act on his divorce petition. They told Milan that they lacked authority. As a last resort, he put pressure on Metropolitan Teodosije, who signed the divorce decree.

The divorce decree, issued in October 1888, placed Milan in an unfavorable light as far as the public was concerned. In the patriarchal Serbia of that day, divorce was looked down upon even when it involved ordinary citizens, let alone the monarch. In addition, the way in which Milan carried out the divorce was but new proof of his unbridled despotic nature. Moreover, for several months matters of state had given way to absorption in matters of his private life.

Victory for Parliamentary Government

Two days after the publication of his divorce decree, Milan ordered elections to take place on November 20, 1888, for the Large National Skupština whose task was to change the constitution. Milan appointed a committee of some eighty leading men from the three political parties to prepare a draft of a new constitution. He retained the presidency of the committee. The basic work was done by a sub-committee of 12 men. Milan exercised a strong leading role in all deliberations. In essence it was the work of Milan, the Belgrade Radicals, and Jovan Ristić. Milan was an effective presiding officer, possessing a combination of patience and decisiveness. He was able rather quickly to find the middle ground, which the parties could accept, and sometimes he virtually forced them to do so. He was able to get the essence of a question after a quick briefing, and he was a gifted speaker. Despite difficulties, he was able to get agreement in the full committee that all members would support the draft without amendments in the constituent assembly.

The constitution was a remarkably democratic document, one of the most liberal constitutions in Europe of that day. In essence, it (1) explicitly established a parliamentary system, (2) strongly protected civil rights, and (3) recognized certain political powers for organs of local government. The unicameral system was retained under the new constitution, but appointive deputies were eliminated. Proportional representation was adopted over the objections of the Radicals because the Liberals and Progressives were adamant on the issue. Ministers could now be members of the Skupština. Milan was not pleased because the monarch was denied any real power.

In the area of civil rights, the constitution was explicit, especially when it came to freedom of the press. Censorship or any prior approval of what was printed were forbidden. The constitution also guaranteed judicial independence, and forbade the setting up summary courts.

The Radicals, who had been the strongest advocates of local self-government and the most bitter critics of bureaucracy, did not get all that they wanted in those areas. Nor did they eliminate the standing army. The increase in the powers of local government, especially when compared with the past, was a big step forward nevertheless.

Ratification by the Large National Skupština came on December 22. Of around 600, the Radicals had about 500, the Liberals about 100, and the Progressives none. The Radicals, who were not happy about some provisions, were told openly and clearly by Milan that they could reject the draft—that was there right—but if they accepted it there could be no changes or additions. Otherwise he would not sign it. In the end, it was adopted with some 75 Radicals voting against it.

Milan's approval of the Constitution of 1888 did not stem from a sudden conversion to democratic parliamentary principles. On the contrary, he was planning to abdicate; what he wanted most of all was the power to appoint the regents who would rule during his son's minority, a power the constitution gave him. Moreover, he was convinced that Serbia was not ready for such a constitution and that it would prove utterly unworkable. He was confident that within two years the ensuing chaos would lead the people, as well as the Great Powers, to beg him to return and restore order. He may have been encouraged in this belief by virtue of the fact that his popularity, so low after his divorce, was in large measure restored by the adoption of the liberal-democratic constitution.

Milan's decision to abdicate was motivated by a number of factors. At different times he gave varied reasons: fear of insanity, marital troubles, the disloyalty of Serbian politicians, and a desire to improve relations with Russia. A letter to German Kaiser Wilhelm II, contains the following revealing paragraph:

> I cannot count on any political party, nor on any man here. It is impossible to rule forever with brutal power; and even the army carries out its duty as a duty, but not with conviction. During these twenty years I have had two revolutions to put down, to say nothing of greater or lesser conspiracies. Over time it becomes repulsive to shoot and imprison men. And every individual who comes out of prison becomes a popular political personality whom everyone likes and respects.

At the same time, we should note that Milan had fallen in love with the wife of his personal secretary, an affair he did not seek to hide. He fully expected her to get a divorce and marry him after his abdication—a forlorn hope as it turned out.

Before abdicating Milan named a three-man regency. He chose Jovan Ristić as first regent although he intensely disliked him. The qualities that recommended Ristić were that he was a seasoned politician and no friend of the Radicals. He had valuable experience as regent during Milan's own minority. Furthermore, he could be pressed into giving Austria-Hungary assurance that Serbia would adhere to the secret treaty of 1881. The other two regents were military men personally loyal to Milan, generals Kosta Protić and Jovan Belimarković.

The principal tasks of the regency, in Milan's view, were three. The first was to protect the dynasty from the Radicals by lulling them asleep politically until the constitution proved unworkable. Secondly, he expected the regency to keep Natalie out of Serbia, particularly since none of the three regents were friendly toward her. Thirdly, Ristić, as the one politician among them, would steer the nation's course politically, while

Milan could continue to mix in Serbian affairs through his two loyal military men, even after his abdication.

At age 35, Milan left the Serbian throne, parliamentarism triumphed, and the Radicals finally came to power. The Constitution of 1888 was the last act in the eight-year struggle between Milan and the Radical party. Ostensibly this was a victory for the latter. In fact, it was only a partial and temporary victory, and Serbia was not to be free of Milan's intrigues until his death in 1901, some twelve years later. His abdication in 1889 was but the end of one chapter in a stormy political saga.

VIII
The Struggle Continues, 1889–1903

The victory for parliamentary government symbolized by the Constitution of 1888 and King Milan's abdication in early 1889 was not to be consolidated until 1903. For several years the parliamentary system worked well, although the continuing quarrel between Milan and Natalie consumed an inordinate amount of time and energy of the political leaders. Just as this problem seemed to have been resolved, a Milan-Alexander duarchy came to dominate Serbian politics for several years. Then followed critical differences between father and son, the assertion of power by Alexander, his unpopular marriage, and the brutal end of the dynasty in 1903, together with the restoration of the Karadjordjević dynasty and the 1888 constitution.

Government Under the Regency, 1889–1893

The Radicals formed the first cabinet under the regency and ushered in several years of stable parliamentary rule. The Radical leaders, most of them first-rate intellectuals (several were subsequently elected to the Serbian Academy of Sciences and Arts), demonstrated that they were responsible and able to perform the tasks of governing. More specifically, they proved: (1) that a certain political stability was attainable, (2) that it was possible to govern constitutionally, and (3) that (1) and (2) could be achieved with Radicals at the helm.

One of the first acts of the new cabinet was to pardon Nikola Pašić, an act recommended by none other than Milan as a "friend" of the regency. Within a few months of his triumphal return, after the landslide victories of the Radicals in the elections of September 1889, Pašić was elected president of the Skupština. It was considered prudent that he not be made prime minister right away, but he headed his first cabinet in February 1891.

Much legislation was needed to implement the new constitution: laws concerning elections, freedom of the press, ministerial responsibility, local government, judiciary, the organization of the army, and others.

In addition, the cabinet made peace with the Orthodox Church and brought back Metropolitan Mihailo as head of the hierarchy.

Aside from enacting laws to implement the new constitution, the Radicals moved quickly in passing certain economic and social measures. One of the first acts was to nationalize the railroads, which was well received at home but not abroad. The necessary agreements were negotiated by October 1889. The operation of the railroads by the government was a success. In addition, the cabinet moved to take over the salt and tobacco monopolies, which had been controlled by foreigners. Furthermore, a state lottery was created, and concessions were provided as a way of encouraging domestic industry. Also laws were passed to protect forests from vandalizing exploitation, to provide "food banks" in the event of bad crop years, and to establish trade and artisan schools.

In the field of foreign affairs, the Radicals experienced tense relations with Austria-Hungary, but contacts with Russia were improved. Relations with Bulgaria presented great difficulties for the Radicals, who realized how badly neglected were the Serbian areas still under Ottoman rule, especially the regions of the old Serbian empire. In those areas the Turks had forbidden Serbian schools but allowed the Bulgarians to move in and to take over Serbian churches and monasteries as well as to establish schools there. The Radical efforts even convinced the Russians, who had supported a Great Bulgaria in the past, that perhaps they should have two irons instead of one in the Balkan fire.

The Radicals had been in power scarcely more than a year when their major efforts were drained off to deal with problems concerning Milan and Natalie. Milan disliked the apparent smooth functioning of the government under the new constitution. In May 1890 he came back to Serbia amid all sorts of rumors about what he was doing. In August he wrote a letter to first regent Ristić which was clearly anti-Radical. Soon thereafter he told Ristić orally: "Give me power, whether in one form or another, so that I can clean up this situation if you will not." To this Ristić replied: "You know that I was the last to agree to your abdication.... If it comes to that, that we have to give up power to someone prior to the constitutional term, then you will not be the one to whom we will give power but to the Large National Skupština." Milan went away angry, but his anger did not hamper his ability to continue plotting.

Natalie, for her part, turned to Metropolitan Mihailo, who had just been returned to his post, and asked that he nullify the earlier divorce decree, and he obliged. The Radical government soon convinced him to rescind his act. Natalie then addressed a memorandum to the Skupština, which found that it was not competent to deal with it. After months of delay and after neither the regents nor the cabinet were able to pacify Natalie, the Radicals decided to sacrifice her. Aided and abetted by mobs of sympathizers, she refused to leave the country. In May 1891, the government put her on a train at night and she was taken out of the country while the city slept. The forcible expulsion was highly unpopular.

Even before Natalie was out of the way, Milan began to bargain with the Radicals. Bruised and annoyed by press stories about his various escapades, he asked the Radicals to change the press law to protect him, and they grudgingly accommodated him. Moreover, he agreed that for a lump sum instead of a monthly allowance, he would leave Serbia until his son was of age. He asked for 6 million dinars, but settled for 1 million plus a promise from the government to find him a loan of an additional 2 million dinars to be secured by his real property in Serbia. The loan was found in Russia, really a gift from the Russian tsar, which was not public information at the time. In return he wrote a letter to the regency renouncing all rights under the constitution, including citizenship and membership in the royal household, as well as the right to educate Alexander. After the Skupština recognized his act, it was made public in March 1892. The Skupština act also stipulated that Milan could not even become a Serbian citizen without its prior approval.

In June 1892, Regent Kosta Protić died suddenly, creating a crisis between the Radicals and first regent Ristić. Under the constitution the Skupština was empowered to fill such a vacancy, but it was not to meet for several months. Pašić recommended a special session, but Ristić would not agree because he feared that Pašić would be elected, thereby overshadowing him. Thereupon Pašić resigned, and Ristić asked a Liberal, Jovan Dj. Avakumović, to form a cabinet, resulting in a bitter struggle between the Radicals and the Liberals. In new elections, held in February 1892, the results were uncertain except that the Radicals had lost their majority. In the end, the Liberals got 69 seats, a scant majority in a body of 134 deputies.

The April 1893 Coup: Alexander in Power, 1893–1897

The somewhat muddled parliamentary situation gave Milan a convenient opportunity to carry out his plans, which had been in the making for several months, to engineer an overthrow of the regency. The coup was bloodless. After a dinner at the palace, to which he had invited the two regents and the ministers, Alexander rose as if to propose a toast. Instead, declaring himself of age (he was not yet 17), he told his honored guests that he had taken the royal powers into his own hands. While they had been dining, troops loyal to Alexander, by prearranged plan, had seized the foreign and interior ministries, the city hall, and the telephone and telegraph companies. Furthermore, the homes of the ministers and regents, as well as the Skupština building, had been surrounded. After his announcement, Alexander left the dining hall while Ristić was beginning to reply. The regents were asked to resign, but refused. Consequently, the king's guests became his prisoners for the night. The next morning found the city plastered with royal decrees, informing the public that Alexander had assumed power.

Milan's motives in engineering the coup were mixed. By 1892 he despaired of the new political system collapsing. The death of regent Protić gave him a pretext for getting involved. These and other political reasons, however, were secondary. His financial needs were uppermost. The sum he received as a lump sum was soon gone. In addition, he pawned his furniture and silver, as well as jewels he had inherited from Prince Mihailo.

In desperation, and completely sacrificing his self-respect, Milan turned to Natalie for help. In a long letter to her in January 1893, he informed her that he was going to commit suicide (but would try to make it seem like an accident), and asked her to give him 345,000 francs so as to pay off his debts and thus avoid leaving a legacy of embarrassment to their son. Natalie took him seriously enough to get together 100,000 francs—all that she could do—but on the condition that he not commit suicide and that he redeem the family jewels and give them to Alexander.

Milan took the money, and faithful to his habits, soon spent it. With the help of his one-time lover, Artemiza, he got a loan from the Sultan of 500,000 francs, paid his debts, but was soon broke again. He quickly realized that his financial woes could be cured only if he could get his hands on some of the unspent money in the civil list. But there were guardians of this money in the palace, and the only way to get it was through a coup. In the hope of helping himself publicly, Milan spread a rumor that there had been a reconciliation with Natalie. He even went so far as to ask the Orthodox Church Council to proclaim the earlier divorce decree null and void, and the Council fulfilled his request in February 1893.

Indeed, the coup was not too unpopular, especially among the Radicals, who were still smarting from Ristić's preventing them from electing a regent the previous year. The first prime minister after the coup was Dr. Lazar Dokić, a professor of anatomy, a one-time tutor of Alexander, and president of the Council of State. A moderate Radical by conviction although not a party member, he managed to get the cooperation of many Radicals, but not that of the party leader, Nikola Pašić, who was sent to Petrograd as Serbia's minister as a means of getting him out of the way. The Liberal-controlled Skupština was dissolved and in new elections the Radicals won all but 10 seats.

Almost immediately, relations between the Radicals and the new monarch began to sour. When Dr. Dokić became ill, there was sharp disagreement as to who should succeed him. Sava Grujić, a moderate Radical who had served under Milan, was appointed prime minister, but his cabinet resigned in January 1895 when Alexander faced them with a fait accompli—he had invited his father to come to Serbia and indeed was on his way.

After Milan's return, Alexander sought to rule through several relatively neutral cabinets. In May 1894, when the Court of Cassation threw out a decree that would have nullified the law that forbade his father's return, Alexander abolished the Constitution of 1888 and returned to the more conservative one of 1869, thus pulling off a coup with the stroke of a pen. This was a hard blow to the Radicals because the Constitution of 1888 symbolized all that they had fought for politically, and because after this second coup there was a systematic elimination of Radicals from the civil service.

The young monarch found himself in the middle—he was getting contradictory advice from his father and his mother. Milan advised governing with any combination except the Radicals, while Natalie argued that the only way to safeguard the dynasty was to work with the Radicals, and in any case not against them. Initially, Alexander leaned towards his father's view, but for about two and a half years (1895–1897), he seemed to be under the influence of his mother. For one thing, by contrast with Milan, she did not want anything for herself. More important, but unknown to Natalie, was her lady-in-waiting, the widow Draga Mašin. Although twelve years older than Alexander, Draga had caught his eye during visits to his mother and he had fallen in love with her.

Nevertheless, Alexander still distrusted the Radicals, partly because they always seemed to be talking about constitutional reform. One of their most gifted polemicists, Stojan Protić, had argued in Radical publications that parliamentary government had to be party government, and that the crown should be above political struggles.

Although Natalie had not fully convinced him to make peace with the Radicals, in December 1896, Alexander entrusted the formation of the cabinet to Djordje Simić, a moderate Radical who a brief time earlier had presided over a politically neutral cabinet. While the second Simić cabinet contained a number of nonpolitical personalities, the Radicals were dominant. Before his appointment of Simić, Alexander had sought and received a promise from the party leader, Pašić, that the constitutional issue would be postponed for a time, ostensibly because of foreign policy problems.

The life of the Simić cabinet was short. It nearly collapsed when Alexander invited his father to come to Belgrade for the Christmas holidays. In June 1897 new elections were held in which the Progressives and Liberals did not take part, with the Radicals winning all the seats. Later in the summer, after a visit with his father abroad, Alexander made a final break with his mother, probably because she was pushing him to marry a European princess, presumably not knowing of his love for Draga. In October he came back to Belgrade with his father, and immediately dismissed the Simić cabinet. This ended the first phase of Alexander's rule after the coup of April 1893, a brief period that witnessed seven separate ministries.

The Milan–Alexander Duarchy: 1897–1900

By contrast with the previous period, the time of the duarchy had only one cabinet, that of Dr. Vladan Djordjević, a renowned surgeon. None of his proposed cabinet appointments, however, was acceptable to the kings. Presiding over a cabinet he did not appoint, he merely acted out the role of prime minister. He and his ministers were not initiators of policies—this was performed by the kings.

This political system was a nonparty personal regime, firm and strict. Consequently, the government ruled without an opposition, and with increasing arrogance. Radicals were purged from the civil service. The press was effectively muzzled and members of the Skupština—chosen by the police instead of by the electorate—did not feel secure and did not dare take issue with positions taken by the ministers or the monarch. The Radicals announced that they would be a loyal opposition, but were frustrated at every turn. Their leader, Pašić, went to jail for several months in 1898 because of a piece in a party publication wherein he admitted that he had opposed Milan. The only opposition that made itself felt came in the way of underground pamphlets and leaflets from abroad, no doubt the work of Radicals.

A few months after taking office, the Djordjević cabinet held new elections in May 1898. The candidates were handpicked from persons known to be loyal to the crown. The Liberals got 112 seats and the Progressives 62. The Radicals got one! The Liberals were still a concern to Alexander and Milan, mainly because Ristić was still their leader. Considerable pressure was exerted on him to give up his post. When he failed to do so, his son was demoted from secretary in the Serbian Legation in Paris to the position of a postman. When this failed to move Ristić, the government put a stop to the Liberal party organ.

The kings were taking no chances in their determination to strengthen the dynasty. From the outset King Father Milan was named commandant of the army, a position he held for two and a half years until an irreparable break with his son. The latter, for his part, introduced medals, autographed portraits, and other ways of buying support, while force as a royal weapon was not relinquished.

As commandant of the army, Milan became a type of state within the state. He saw to it that large sums were spent on building up the army, and even cabinet ministers dared not to discuss the army budget or other military matters. Milan took his duties seriously and was popular with the officers. He was not an expert in military matters, but he quickly grasped the main needs and subordinated everything else to them.

The politically neutral Skupština passed a large number of constructive laws, but it also severely limited the press, and in effect abolished political parties. The regime introduced reforms in the school system and in the bureaucracy with the aim of preventing penetration by allegedly subversive elements. Usually, the special target was the Radical party and its friends.

In foreign affairs, the cabinet and the two kings were caught in a diplomatic crossfire between Austria-Hungary and Russia. The two powers had reached an agreement in 1897 to respect the status quo in the Balkans, but both tried to undermine each other. Alexander hoped to improve relations between Russia and his father, but this was to no avail. Relations continued to be excellent with Vienna during the Djordjević ministry.

Toward the end of the Djordjević ministry, two major events shook Serbia and, to a degree, Europe as well. The first was the attempt on Milan's life in June 1899, for which the Radicals were blamed and as a result of which at least two of their leaders escaped death sentences only through foreign interventions. The second, a year later, was Alexander's decision to marry Draga Mašin, causing a final break with his father, who left Serbia never to return.

There is still a great deal of dispute as to the attempt on Milan's life, with some allegations that the whole affair was staged so as to provide the government with a pretext to act against the Radicals. In any event, the very evening it happened an order went out from the palace to arrest Pašić, who had just returned from a nine-month prison sentence, and other Radicals. The next day a massive persecution of Radicals began, and a summary court was created to try the accused. Milan was insistent that at least Pašić and Kosta Taušanović, another member of the Radical Main Committee, must be sentenced to death. Fortunately for the two of them. Russia and Austria-Hungary stepped in to save them. While the trial was in progress, Vienna sent her military attaché to inform Milan and Alexander that they could not execute Pašić and Taušanović else the dynasty would be boycotted by all of Europe.

Milan sent the minister of interior, Djordje Genčić, to the Belgrade prison in an effort to make a deal with Pašić. In return for an admission that he had tolerated anti-dynastic elements in the party, Pašić could save his life and that of other Radicals. Not knowing that his life had already been saved, Pašić agreed. As a consequence, Pašić became the most unpopular man in the country, a factor that triggered a split in the Radical party.

The summary court sentenced two men to death: the would-be assassin and an associate who had fled abroad. It convicted 15 Radicals, most of whom got 20-year prison terms. Pašić and Taušanović were tried separately, with Pašić getting five years and Taušanović eight. Pašić was immediately pardoned and Taušanović's term reduced to three years. No real proof had been produced in any of the cases.

The other event that shook Serbia in the last year of the Djordjević cabinet was Alexander's decision to marry Draga, a widow over ten years his senior. When informed of his desire, the cabinet resigned. This was in July 1900. Earlier in the year the young king informed his father that he would marry a German princess. When news of the "bolt out of the blue" reached Milan, who was abroad, he wrote to his son, resigning his position as commandant of the army. As a parting shot, he wrote: "If this decision of yours is irrevocable, as you say, then there is nothing left for me but to pray for the fatherland. After this impulsive act, I would be the first to greet the government which would overthrow you."

Alexander's decision was not generally popular, and had Milan given the word, the army would probably have dethroned him. Alexander must have had some fears, because he gave orders that his father should be stopped if he should attempt to return. Alexander also could not find any known politician to form a "wedding" cabinet. Also, no general would accept the position of minister of war. On the day that he announced a wedding cabinet, Alexander pardoned all the Radicals who had been convicted of the attempt to assassinate his father a year earlier.

A few days after the marriage, and after the initial shock and disbelief, public opinion began to change. More and more people began to say that a native wife was better than a German princess. The opinion was no doubt reinforced by the news that the Russian tsar had agreed to become the godfather, and the realization that Milan's influence in Serbia was finally at an end. Ironically, Milan died a few months later in Vienna, a grieving and dejected "old man" who had not yet reached his 47th birthday.

The Last Days of Alexander's Reign

Milan's death in January 1901 lifted the burden of fear from the royal couple. During the previous several months, Milan's friends and Draga's enemies were purged from government service, especially from the army. With the fear of Milan removed, Alexander turned to other problems. And the Radicals became bolder and began to raise the constitutional question which the monarch managed to delay and evade.

At first Alexander was successful in promoting a Radical-Progressive agreement, which led to a new constitution. The first cabinet under this arrangement was headed by Radical Mihailo Vujić. And Alexander octroyed the new constitution, which brought some liberalization, but as a half-measure it whetted the appetite for political freedoms. Soon the Radical-Progressive agreement was at an end. In elections in July 1901, the Radicals demonstrated their strength, but were given only three cabinet posts. After several cabinet crises, a new ministry was appointed in October 1902 under the leadership of Pera Velimirović, but this was a poorer edition of the Vujić ministry. It fell within a month, which ended the Radical-Progressive agreement and Alexander returned to a personal regime.

One consequence of the Radical-Progressive agreement was to augment the division in the Radical ranks. Already alienated to a degree because of Pašić's "cowardly" behavior before the summary court, the younger Radicals, in the main lawyers and professors, criticized the agreement as a retreat from the Radical party program. And while the Radicals managed to hold their own in the 1901 elections, the Independent Radicals were to stay as a separate political party.

Alexander's return to personal rule did not solve his problems. A month after his marriage it was announced that the queen was pregnant, and when this news turned out to be false and a deliberate ruse, the public was not amused. Nor were people pleased by Draga's apparent domination over the young monarch. Not only was her birthday celebrated in grand style, but in addition her name was given to army regiments, schools, and peasant villages.

Stung by items appearing in the press, in March 1903 Alexander suspended the constitution for forty-five minutes in the middle of the night. During that brief period several laws that permitted a relatively free press and other political activities were repealed or amended, and the more stringent laws from an earlier period were reenacted. The new elections held in early May were boycotted by most political groups and no opposition deputies were elected.

Meanwhile, dissatisfaction with Alexander's regime had been growing. This was especially true in the army, where even young officers had come to believe that Alexander's marriage to Draga, whom they regarded as a woman with a promiscuous past, had brought dishonor to the whole officer corps. Adding to their attitude was the fact that material conditions in the army deteriorated sharply after Milan's departure. Finally, the opposition press tended to incite the officers.

In late May 1903, a conspiracy that had been in the making for two years resulted in the assassination of Alexander and Draga. Initially, the conspiracy was the work of young officers, who constantly widened their circle. Since they did not have any particular political orientation, they involved a small number of civilians, but no known Radicals or Karadjordjević followers. The officers viewed their task as getting rid of the king and the queen. The task of the civilians was to choose a new king and a new prime minister. Alexander did not understand the nature or strength of officer dissatisfaction. He viewed the news of a possible conspiracy as an effort to create a quarrel between him and the army. In addition to Alexander and Draga, the conspirators also killed the prime minister and the minister of war, while the minister of interior was seriously wounded. There was no plan to kill any ministers; this was decided upon hastily after the palace had been entered and when for a time Alexander and Draga were nowhere to be found. The death of the royal couple marked the extinction of the Obrenović dynasty and the end of a twenty-year struggle between this dynasty and the Radical party.

IX

Return of Parliamentary Rule, 1903–1918

The year 1903 opened an extraordinary decade for Serbia, a decade that saw the return of parliamentary rule. It was also a decade characterized by economic growth and a renaissance in the fields of education, literature, and the arts. It was a time of balanced budgets. It was also a period of domestic and foreign troubles. There were considerable territorial gains as a result of the Balkan wars against the decaying Ottoman empire. But it was also the time when the Austro-Hungarian rulers sought to prevent the Serbs from realizing some of these gains, finally declaring war on them in 1914. The end of the war in 1918 found the Serbs uniting with their brethren in Montenegro, Bosnia-Hercegovina, Vojvodina, and with other South Slavs to form the Kingdom of the Serbs, Croats, and Slovenes, later to be known as Yugoslavia.

Return of Parliamentary Rule

The conspirators who ended the Obrenović dynasty turned power over to an all-party coalition, which legitimized the return of parliamentary rule by calling into session the parliament that had been chosen under the Constitution of 1901. The parliament merely ratified previously agreed-upon acts—mainly the choice of Peter Karadjordjević as king and the return of the democratic Constitution of 1888, now to be known as the Constitution of 1903. With these changes Serbia again became a constitutional parliamentary monarchy.

The new king was the grandson of the leader of the first Serbian revolt against the Turks in 1804. Aside from the Karadjordjević name, Peter had a number of qualities that endeared him to his fellow Serbs. He had translated John Stuart Mill's essay *On Liberty* into Serbian, prefaced with an introduction permeated with the spirit of democracy. This had been circulated widely, though surreptitiously, in Serbia. In the Franco-Prussian war of 1870 he had fought in the French army and was wounded. In 1876 he had fought, under the name Petar Mrkonjić, in the Serbian uprising against the Turks in Bosnia-Hercegovina, a popular and courageous act. As king, he not only became a constitutional monarch, but also earned the love and respect of the people by his modest and frugal way of life, thus becoming a true son of a people who still had a long way to go in economic development.

Although the Constitution of 1903 restored a free and vigorous political life, Serbia's new leaders were determined to strengthen the nation's constitutional order through important reforms. The constitution was amended so as to give the cabinet control over finance, making it impossible for the Skupština to engage in irresponsible acts. In addition, a Court of Accounts, whose members were chosen for life by the Skupština, was established as a type of controller, serving as an independent check on the validity of government expenditures. Moreover, to secure the rule of law, the independence of the judiciary was guaranteed by making judges irremovable. Finally, a system of administrative courts was created, with the Council of State as the supreme administrative tribunal, as an easy and inexpensive way that citizens could challenge acts of government officials which they believed to be contrary to the law.

Political decision-making was left to the people's representatives in the Skupština. These were chosen in hotly contested elections, mainly between the Radicals and the Independent Radicals (or just Independents). The other parties that had played a role in the latter part of the nineteenth century—the Liberals and the Progressives—had spent themselves in power and had finished their historical missions with the end of the Obrenović era.

The Radicals, who had the support of the masses, developed an internal split at the turn of the century. The rift stemmed in large part from the dissatisfaction of vigorous intellectuals with the party's leaders, mainly Nikola Pašić. They were horrified with what they regarded as Pašić's cowardice before the summary court in 1899, when his life was at stake. Many also felt that Pašić was old and not energetic enough, and some of the intellectuals looked down upon his peasant background. The intellectuals believed that they should inherit the leadership, in part because of their courageous opposition during the last years of Alexander's reign. When they realized that Pašić was beginning to rehabilitate himself through various compromises, most of them believed that they were on the way to forming a new political party. But in the years after 1903, while always a serious challenge to the Radicals, the Independents had insufficient strength at the polls.

The first elections under a new constitution, held in September 1903, did not give any party a majority. Consequently, a coalition of Radicals and Independents formed a cabinet under the leadership of Sava Grujić, a moderate and conciliatory Radical. The cabinet was unable to resolve basic disagreements over finance, the building of new railroads, rearmament, and relations with the military. In November 1903, the cabinet was replaced by the Radical leader, Pašić. He built a small majority by getting the leader of the Independents, Ljuba Živković, and a few others to return to the Radical fold. The remaining Independents elected a new leader, Ljuba Stojanović.

Confronted by parliamentary obstructionist tactics on the part of the Independents, Pašić resolved to improve upon his slender majority through new elections. King Peter, however, refused his request for a dissolution and new elections, possibly the one unparliamentary act of his reign. Pašić resigned. The king then appointed Stojanović as prime minister and almost immediately granted his request for new elections. This act on the part of the monarch—to refuse Pašić's request and then to grant it to his successor—seemed contrary to traditional parliamentary practice and was widely criticized in the Radical press. After a hard fought campaign, the Independents won 81 out of 160 parliamentary seats, the slenderest possible majority.

The Stojanović cabinet was in power for less than a year. Its prestige and authority were undermined by its attempt to conclude a loan with a Viennese bank and to negotiate an arms purchase agreement with Austro-Hungarian firms. In view of Serbia's past difficulties with Austria-Hungary, these plans received a hostile public reception. The Skupština's refusal to approve the loan agreement led to Stojanović's resignation, and the king's turn to the Radicals, who in the April 1906 elections won a solid majority. The Independents never recovered. From that time until the formation of Yugoslavia in December 1918, the Radicals were in power, with Pašić as prime minister most of the time. After Vienna's declaration of war on Serbia in 1914, an all-party coalition cabinet under Pašić was formed, but the coalition came apart in 1917, of which more will be said subsequently.

Domestic Political Struggles

In the course of the decade prior to World War I, Serbia's relatively new and hard-won democratic political system was confronted with a number of thorny domestic problems. These had to be handled in the context of a great deal of inexperience, and even intolerance, among the politicians, to say nothing of the slender Radical majorities. And they had to be considered along with ambitious programs in the social, economic, and cultural fields. Moreover, the troublesome domestic questions were not unrelated to the difficulties in the foreign realm.

Perhaps the most critical domestic questions were: (1) the sensitive matter of the conspirators who overthrew the Obrenović dynasty, (2) the need for foreign loans, mainly for rearmament, (3) the abdication of Prince George, the heir to the throne, and (4) the problem of civil-military relations. The first two were of immediate concern, the third was not long in coming, and the fourth evolved more or less gradually. The Pašić cabinet succeeded in finding solutions to the first three, but the fourth continued to plague the king and the cabinet into the World War I years, and led finally to the trial and conviction of several army officers in 1917.

Much of Europe was horrified by the brutal assassination of the Obrenovićes, and the new Serbian king was publicly attacked in some foreign newspapers for surrounding himself with murderers. Great Britain broke diplomatic relations and demands were heard in many foreign circles for punishment of the conspirators. King Peter was uneasy because, after all, the conspirators had brought him to the throne. And the conspirators added to the problem. Instead of abiding by their oath that if the conspiracy succeeded they would not seek personal rewards, they (about 60 in number) sought to make themselves bosses of the army and to be influential at the palace. In that way they created a gulf between themselves and the experienced politicians in the parliamentary regime.

Since in Serbia punishment could not even be mentioned, seemingly the only way out was to pension the conspirators, a solution acceptable to the British and certain other foreign circles. King Peter was at first opposed, believing that this was a drastic solution to a delicate matter. He preferred a voluntary agreement by which the conspirators would step down, but they were not cooperative. Prime Minister Pašić, however, was unwavering, cool, and logical. Through long and patient talks, he got the older conspirators to retire by giving them full pay, and the king approved. Although this was not strictly legal, it was a way of resolving a difficult question without quarrels and without scandal. The younger officers, who at that time were not involved in politics, were allowed to remain on active service, with the understanding that they would not get involved in politics. The fact that they failed to abide by this understanding was to continue as a source of latent conflict between the civil and military authority.

The question of Serbia's rearmament was critical on two counts: (1) the Radical cabinet was determined that the state budget should be balanced, and was, which meant that foreign loans were needed if the army was to be modernized, and (2) Austria-Hungary wanted to be the lender as a way of making Serbia dependent on Vienna both politically and economically. As pointed out above, the Independents had negotiated a loan and an arms purchase agreement with Vienna but this was rejected by the Skupština. Pašić's Radical cabinet was convinced that Serbia must seek to liberate itself from dependence on Vienna. At the same time, Pašić knew that it would be suicidal to get involved militarily with Austria.

The Austro-Hungarian leaders were convinced that Serbia had no choice because they could interrupt Serbia's foreign trade, most of which was with the dual monarchy. This position was also shared by Serbian economic experts. Pašić, for his part, gave oral promises that he was willing to conclude agreements with Vienna, but delayed matters until opposition in the Skupština to such agreements could increase. When Austria demanded that the question be resolved, Pašić indicated his willingness but pointed out that the Skupština was opposed. Thereupon the Austrian leaders lost their patience and closed its borders to Serbia's trade. Pašić had risked a tariff war, and now he had it, but he did not waver. His response was to conclude a loan in France and to purchase cannons for the Serbian army from French firms. Although the tariff war lasted several years and caused Serbia serious economic difficulties, the decisiveness of the Pašić cabinet promoted Serbia's political and economic independence.

The abdication in March 1909 of Prince George, the heir to the throne, came about as a result of several factors. The immediate cause was the death of his orderly, whom George had kicked in the stomach because George suspected that he was an instrument of his enemies. More important were his anti-parliamentary statements, especially his enmity toward the Radical leader, Pašić. Also contributing to his abdication were his war-like statements to the foreign and domestic press at the time of the Bosnia-Hercegovina annexation crisis (1908–1909).

It cannot be said that George did not know what he was doing. He admitted that his father and others had told him what his proper role should be in a constitutional monarchy. Among other things, his father told him that "a king does not dare to disagree with his ministers. For him they represent the people, and the people's will is law." These admonitions had little impact on George. Subsequently, he admitted that he told his father openly that he would never collaborate with Pašić. This haughty attitude toward the essence of the parliamentary system was compounded by his unconstitutional attempt to communicate directly with the Skupština. Even after his abdication, George could not refrain from criticizing Pašić, at least to his father and his brother Alexander, who was the new heir to the throne.

The question of the relationship of the civil and military authority had its inception in the pensioning of the officer-conspirators in 1906, discussed above. The hostility toward Pašić and the Radicals that it produced in army ranks might have faded with the years had it not been for Austria-Hungary's increasing threat to Serbia's national security. This threat was made evident by Vienna's tariff war and by its annexation of largely Serbian lands of Bosnia-Hercegovina, as well as by the hostility toward Serbia in the Austro-Hungarian press. One reaction to this threat was the creation in Serbia of patriotic societies with an increasing affinity for the military. One of these, the "Union or Death" group (sometimes referred to as the "Black Hand"), was a secret revolutionary organization whose primary base was officers in the army. Their aim was to work toward the union of Serbian lands by whatever means necessary. In setting this task for the organization, its leaders were in effect taking unto themselves an attribute of state power, contrary to the basic principles of a constitutional state and in fundamental conflict with military laws.

For some time, the conflict between the civil and military authority was subdued, but soon after the Balkan wars (1912–1913) it was brought out into the open in veiled exchanges between the publications of the Black Hand and the Radical party. The bone of contention was the Pašić cabinet's desire to place the newly-liberated territories under civilian rule at an early date. After Pašić's cabinet issued an official order that the civil authority had priority, the commandant in Skoplje refused and was promptly dismissed. The moving force in the Union or Death, Colonel Dragutin Dimitrijević-Apis, even suggested to some of his military colleagues that it would be a good thing if some of the civilian administrators were forced to leave for home with all their baggage.

The response of the Pašić cabinet was to retire or transfer many of the officer-conspirators, but the situation had become complicated by the fact that some of the Independents had joined the fray in a desire to exploit the conflict to their own advantage. Articles criticizing the cabinet written by Pašić's opponents appeared in the Union or Death publication. King Peter, who may have been inclined toward the Independents, asked Pašić to change certain provisions in the cabinet decree concerning the priority of the civil authority, but the cabinet stood firm. Pašić, believing that it was desirable to put the issue to the voters, especially since he had a majority of only seven votes in the Skupština, submitted his resignation and asked for dissolution of the cabinet and new elections.

Many expected the monarch to turn to the Independents, but he was willing to do so only if they could fashion a coalition cabinet, which proved impossible. Moreover, he got indications from the French and the Russians that they had confidence only in Pašić. Thereupon the king granted Pašić's request, and almost immediately transferred the royal powers to his son Alexander. The latter act probably stemmed from his inability or unwillingness to deal decisively with the civil-military conflict.

Serbia's outstanding military victories against the Austro-Hungarian forces in the first year of the war resulted in a great deal of domestic tranquility. Her defeats in the fall of 1915 and the terrible and costly withdrawal through the Albanian mountains in winter, however, rekindled the conflict. Many officers believed that the tragedy could have been averted had Pašić permitted them to attack the Bulgarian forcers in a move to get to the Greek port of Salonika. But since the allies were still hoping to win Bulgaria over to their side, Pašić had not wanted to incur Russia's wrath by attacking the Bulgarians. In exile on the Greek island of Corfu, Colonel Apis and his collaborators made no secret of their hostility toward Pašić and the Radicals. One of them even suggested that the latter would ultimately have to return to the homeland through "the gate of swords." The challenge to the civil authority was clear.

When Serbian forces were on their way back to Serbia, Colonel Apis and some twenty collaborators were arrested in December 1916 and tried before a military court in June 1917 and convicted. Nine were sentenced to be shot, three of whom were actually executed, among them Apis. The main charge against the group was that they had been responsible for an attempt on Alexander's life and of conspiring to overthrow the duly constituted government. Whatever one thinks of the evidence presented, the appropriateness of the penalties, or the motives of the principals on both sides, it is clear that Alexander and Pašić—who had no love for each other—were in agreement that some settling of accounts between the civil authority and the military authority could not be avoided or long delayed. And whatever one thinks of their judgment, there seems little doubt that Apis and his collaborators exceeded the proper role of the military in a democratic political system.

Foreign Affairs Problems

In the decade prior to World War I, Serbia's foreign affairs difficulties were almost exclusively with Austria-Hungary. The leaders in Vienna believed that a truly independent Serbia would be a threat to the dual monarchy because Serbia would gain strength as she annexed Serbian areas of the decaying Ottoman Empire, and a strong Serbia would constitute a powerful attraction to the South Slav inhabitants in Austria-Hungary. The Viennese rulers concluded, therefore, that Serbia should be prevented from annexing areas under Turkish rule, that she must not be allowed to join hands with the other Serbian state, Montenegro, and that she must not be permitted access to the Adriatic Sea.

To achieve these objectives, and correspondingly to strengthen her position in the Balkans, Austria-Hungary undertook three major actions. These were: (1) a tariff war against Serbia when the latter refused to accept an economically dependent position, (2) the outright annexation of Bosnia-Hercegovina, and (3) a projected railroad across the Sandjak of Novipazar, a narrow strip of land separating Serbia and Montenegro. When these actions proved insufficient to weaken Serbia, Vienna sought (in the main successfully) to deny to Serbia and Montenegro significant fruits of their victories in the Balkan wars of 1912–1913. Even this was not enough. Consequently, the rulers in Vienna decided on an outright military attack, which came in the summer of 1914.

As noted earlier, the tariff war lasted from 1906 to 1911, and did not have the effect that Vienna desired. The task of finding new outlets for Serbia's trade was not easy for a government operating a relatively new and fragile democratic political system, but in the end victory was achieved. The tariff war tested the resourcefulness of the Serbs, strengthened their self-confidence, and lifted their morale. While plans for promoting Serbia's economic growth had to be curtailed during the tariff war, in the process doors were opened to new foreign capital, which in the end contributed significantly to Serbia's economic development.

In the annexation of Bosnia-Hercegovina, however, the dual monarchy had its way. Austria-Hungary had been given the right to occupy and administer the region by the Congress of Berlin (1878), but not to annex it. By 1908, however, she had gone a long way toward getting German and Russian blessings for the annexation. The announcement of the actual act in October of that year came while Serbian leaders were preoccupied with the tariff war. For Serbia, the annexation struck at vital national interests more than the tariff war, and the reaction among the people was in the nature of a suicidal frenzy, demanding war. The Serbian leaders, however, knew that little Serbia could do no more than protest. Serbia's stand was juridically unassailable; France, Russia, and England agreed, but were unwilling to act. Russia even exerted pressure on the Serbian government, forcing it to declare in writing that Serbia's rights were not impaired by the annexation and agreeing to cease further protests.

Austria's plan to annex Bosnia-Hercegovina and to build a railroad across Novipazar were planned at about the same time, with the latter due to come first. Austria-Hungary's presence in Novipazar was based on the Treaty of Berlin, as indicated above, and she was anxious to gain the right to build the railroad before she would tear up that Treaty with the annexation. By controlling a piece of territory stretching from Bosnia-Hercegovina to Salonika, Vienna would have direct access to Bulgaria and would encircle Serbia and keep her from reaching the Adriatic, Montenegro, or even Greece. When the railway project was announced in January 1908, there was a general public outcry in Europe. Serbia's leaders at that time engaged in talks with Vienna concerning a new trade agreement, did not protest publicly. Subsequently, the Young Turk revolution in Turkey doomed the project, and Vienna was thereby spared considerable embarrassment.

At about the time that the tariff war ended (1911), the Balkan nations were working on an agreement (actually signed early in 1912) to liberate their region from Turkish control. War broke out in October 1912 and the Turks met a quick defeat. This came as a surprise to most of Europe and especially to the leaders in Vienna, who had anticipated that Turkey would administer a defeat to the upstart Balkan nations. Responding to Turkey's call for intervention by the Great Powers, Austria-Hungary demanded that Serbian and Montenegrin forces be compelled to withdraw—they had both driven to the Adriatic. The Serbian leader, Pašić, was in a difficult spot; the people and army officers were publicly defiant. But since the Russian foreign minister, Sazanov, promised to defend Serbia's interests, Pašić placed the matter in the hands of the Great Powers. Much to the chagrin of Montenegro's and Serbia's leaders, the Great Powers decided to create an Albanian state on the Adriatic, denying to the Serbian states their hard-fought victories.

Serbia also had difficulties with Bulgaria as to where their new boundaries should lie. In their agreement before entering the war against Turkey, the two nations had agreed that the Russian Tsar would arbitrate in case of unresolved conflict. Since Bulgaria seemed in no mood to seek a peaceful solution, concentrating its troops on Serbia's borders, Pašić finally agreed to ask the Russian Tsar to arbitrate, although he was apprehensive because of Russia's past pro-Bulgarian policy. With great difficulty, he got the approval of the Skupština in support of his position. While still in the Skupština, he received the news that the Bulgarian forces had launched an attack against Serbia on several fronts. Fortunately for Serbia, the Bulgarians had also alienated Romania and Greece, who came to Serbia's side. Within a month the Bulgarians were defeated and a peace treaty was signed in Bucharest in August 1913.

Serbia's prime minister, Nikola Pašić, was more perceptive than other European leaders in his conviction that the rulers in Vienna were planning additional hostile acts against his country. In the early spring of 1914, he expressed his fears personally to the Russian Tsar in Petrograd and asked for his help in case of an Austro-Hungarian attack. The Tsar was incredulous, but Pašić reviewed in detail the events of the previous several years, arguing that the Vienna rulers considered these events as defeats and would engage in other actions, including military attack. The Tsar listened but was still disbelieving. In the end, he promised Russian protection in case of an unprovoked attack. With this assurance, Pašić decided to hold new elections in the summer, particularly since the elections of 1912 had given his party an exceedingly narrow majority.

Pašić's fears proved justified. The Austro-Hungarian leaders decided that a preventive war against Serbia was an absolute necessity for the salvation of the dual monarchy and succeeded in convincing their allies in Berlin of that position. This was before the assassination in Sarajevo of the heir to the Austrian throne in June 1914, which the Viennese leaders used as a pretext a month later to declare war on Serbia. While the assassination was the work of Austria's Serbian subjects in Bosnia-Hercegovina, there has been no proof that the Serbian government had any knowledge of the assassination plans, let alone having any part in them. Nevertheless, on July 23 Vienna presented the Serbs with an unbelievably humiliating 48-hour ultimatum, drafted in such a way that Serbia could not accept it and still remain an independent state.

Most Serbian politicians, including Pašić, were on the campaign trail when the ultimatum was presented in Belgrade. In no position to go to war with anyone, Serbia's leaders were compelled to accept practically all the demands, and expressed a willingness to refer the other matters to the International Court at The Hague. Indicative of how little Vienna was interested in the Serbian answer is the fact that after a hasty reading of the note that Pašić had handed him, the Austro-Hungarian minister declared that diplomatic relations between their two countries were being broken. Moreover, he and his staff, bags already packed, were on the evening train two hours after Pašić had handed him the Serbian answer.

No one had expected little Serbia to be much of a match for the Austrian empire. Yet the latter's armies, after some initial victories, were badly beaten by the Serbs in several important battles. In less than a year all Serbian soil was cleared of the enemy. But in the summer of 1915, a coordinated German-Austrian campaign (subsequently joined by Bulgaria) was launched against the Serbian forces, compelling them to withdraw. Ultimately the remnants of the Serbian armies made their way across the Albanian mountains in the winter of 1915–1916, ending up on the Greek island of Corfu. There were heavy losses of men and materiel, made worse by the terrible epidemic of typhus. By April 1916, however, the Serbs (with Allied help) had re-equipped an army of some 115,000 men, which was sent to the Salonika front. It should also be noted that it was on Corfu that the basic agreements were reached concerning the creation of Yugoslavia, which was consummated on December 1, 1918, and subsequently gained widespread recognition in the Versailles peace settlement.

It is interesting to note that in a brief historical period Serbia made great strides toward consolidating a liberal-democratic political system. In the decade before the First World War constitutional liberals and parliamentary supremacy made greater headway in Serbia than in other European countries, except that certain countries, such as Great Britain, must be excluded from any such comparison. According to John Reed, a leading United States newsman who was there during part of the First World War, Serbia was "one of the most democratic [countries] in the world. It is governed by the Skouptchina, a one-chamber parliament elected by universal suffrage...the present king is strictly a figurehead, limited by a liberal constitution."[1] And her progress was achieved at a

---

[1] *The War in Eastern Europe: Travels Through the Balkans in 1915* (London: Orion House, 1916), pp. 23-24.

time of difficult domestic and foreign problems. To be sure, cabinets were characterized by an element of instability, as in France, with the average life of a cabinet being eight and one-half months. It should be noted, however, new cabinets were often reshuffles of previous ones, with the principal personalities continuing for longer periods of time. All things considered, political democracy was in a state of excellent health in pre-World War I Serbia.

X

Serbia in the First Yugoslavia

In the decade before the First World War, the Serbs had reason to feel pretty good. Their major achievement, a solid parliamentary democracy was the culmination of long, difficult, and costly sacrifices. They were finally rid of the dynasty (Obrenović) that had for decades stood in their way, and the restoration of the dynasty (Karadjordjević) that promised that the monarch would stand above political battles. In King Peter they had the ideal who had previously translated John Stuart Mill's essay *On Liberty* into Serbian.

And the success of Serbia and its Balkan neighbors in the Balkan wars against Turkey was a culmination of their dreams of forcing the Turks to leave Europe. For the Serbs the liberation of Kosovo was the revenge for 1389. To be sure, the refusal of the Great Powers to let Serbia and Montenegro keep all their gains was a great disappointment. Austria-Hungary's annexation of Bosnia-Hercegovina was also a terrible blow.

Moreover, there were serious economic and social problems, but some progress had been made. All in all, comparing the situation—foreign and domestic—at the beginning of the decade and at its end, the Serbs had reason to be proud, if not completely satisfied.

Ideas Toward a Larger South Slav State

The peoples of the Balkans were slow in realizing their national ambitions, due in large part to the actions of five empires (Ottoman, Austro-Hungarian, Russian, French, and to a lesser extent British) that found their respective interests in conflict in that part of the world. Because of selfish interests, they helped to keep the local inhabitants in the dark, educating only those who could become their agents. By the time that the nineteenth century had arrived, however, one thing was clear: the Balkan masses could no longer be kept in the dark.

In the latter part of the nineteenth century, some South Slavs (Serbs in Serbia and Montenegro) had their own states, while others (Croats, Slovenes, and a large number of Serbs) lived under foreign rule, mainly Austro-Hungarian and Turkish. While Serbs, Croats, and Slovenes had common ethnic roots and in large part a common language, there were divisive factors. The foreign rulers made use of the divisive factors to sow seeds of distrust. Religion was divisive; the Serbs were mainly Orthodox, while Croats and Slovenes were mostly Roman Catholic. Another divisive and complicating factor was the significant number of Serbs and Croats who had accepted the Muslim faith during the long years of Turkish occupation. Confessional boundaries, therefore, tended to divide the South Slavs even before there was national awareness. And when that awareness came, the Yugoslav idea had to compete with pan-Serb and pan-Croat ideas.

Social differences were also important. Serbian society was peasant and patriarchal, but without superstructure. Croatian society, on the other hand, had many attributes of a class society. The Croats had made accommodations to Vienna and Budapest. They promoted the study of Hungarian in Croatian schools. Slovene society was also a class society, one in which Germanization had made great inroads. In both Croat and Slovene areas there was an effort to show how the Croats and Slovenes differed from the Serbs, painting the latter as backward Balkan types. These were but some of the difficulties and complexities that confronted those who espoused the idea of a Yugoslav state. In spite of all the difficulties—real or perceived—there were dreamers among the South Slavs who were not to be deterred. These were mainly Croat and Serb intellectuals who struck a responsive chord with idealistic youth. The peasant masses generally did not engage in the romantic emotionalism of the Yugoslav idea. Yet the intellectuals were not operating in a vacuum. These were people-to-people contacts, especially in the border areas, where people crossed boundaries to go to church services, athletic events, and other outings. Serbian singing societies and gymnastic events brought different South Slavs together. Such mingling encouraged intellectuals to push toward the realization of their idea.

The question of who brought forth the idea of a South Slav or Yugoslav state would require a book-length treatise at least. There were many visionaries among the Croat and Serbian intelligentsia. In the beginning, the variations on the South Slav idea were nebulous and, perhaps for that reason, evoked no disagreements. When more specific proposals were made, differences began to appear. This was not surprising since Serbs lived in five of the South Slav territories, the Croats in three, and the others in one each. This suggested that territory—like religion, historical experience, and social values—could not be a sound basis for South Slav unity. The one common denominator was language, but how great a unifier was language? What other matters played roles?

What of the views of those who aspired to be political leaders? Those in Serbia viewed Belgrade as the natural capital of all South Slavs. Many in Croatia, especially those living along the Adriatic, distrusted Serbs and looked to Zagreb as the natural center. In these areas, as well as in Slovenia, there was respect for authority and for government functionaries generally. The Serbs, on the other hand, tended to distrust authority, especially when identified with titled person. In effect, there were two sets of values, two philosophies, two civilizations. In general, the peasant masses did not engage in the emotionalism of the Yugoslav idea, and the two intelligentsias—Serb and Croat—that were to be the main creators of Yugoslavia were to find themselves far apart at critical moments.

Contributing to what were to become serious rifts among the Serbs, Croats, and Slovenes, were their different historical, state-legal, and cultural traditions. Serbia fought for and won its independence and therefore struggled for democracy and established a constitutional parliamentary system. The Croats and Slovenes, on the other hand, were under Austria-Hungary and did not have their own political institutions. The peasant in Serbia had his own leaders, those who had led him against the Turks and later went into the elected parliaments. While the Serbian peasant was forcing the ruler to leave the throne, his Croatian counterpart seemed powerless against local officials, let alone any of those at the top. This great variance in political development and experience of the Serbian masses and those under Austria-Hungary could not but have a negative impact on any effort to create a common state.

Although Croats and Slovenes, unlike the Serbs, did not have their own national parliaments, they did have political groups or parties in which Serbs from those areas participated. In the ranks of these parties came some early divisions between Serbs and Croats, which contributed to future difficulties. In Serbia political parties differed in terms of ideas and programs. They did not divide along nationality lines. In Croatia, however, they divided along Serbian or Croatian orientations, toward Belgrade or Zagreb.

Toward Unification

All the foregoing was and is interesting, and might have remained just that, interesting—had it not been for the fortuitous confluence of three indispensable circumstances in 1914: (1) the desire of the South Slavs to unite, (2) the decay of the Ottoman Empire, and (3) the dissolution of the Habsburg Empire.

Regarding the first of these, as discussed above, the supporters of Yugoslav unity stressed the fact that the people had much in common—language first of all. They increasingly pointed with pride to Serbia, which in the nineteenth century had regained its independence and rapidly developed a parliamentary democratic system that, in 1903, was unmatched on the European continent except perhaps in France and one or two small countries in Western Europe. Consequently, Serbia was a political magnet for the Slovenes, Croats, and Serbs still living under foreign rule.

The second prerequisite for the formation of South Slav state, the decay and disintegration of the Ottoman Empire, was well on its way before the turn of the century. In the Balkan wars of 1912, Serbia and its allies drove the Ottoman Turks out of Europe.

The third circumstance that would make possible the creation of Yugoslav state, the dismemberment of the Habsburg empire, seemed merely a dream before the First World War, and even when war broke out, the dissolution of that empire was far from certain.

The First World War

Despite the odds, soon after Austria's attack on Serbia in 1914, the Serbian cabinet, under the leadership of Prime Minister Pašić, declared in December that its major war aim, after victory, was the liberation and unification of all Serbs, Croats, and Slovenes. Regarded by some as an act of bravado, the declaration was confirmed by the Serbian parliament, and the message was conveyed to Serbia's allies. This war aim soon ran counter to the policies of the Entente Powers. In 1915, they concluded the Secret Treaty of London, whereby they induced Italy to leave the Triple Alliance and to join them. In order to do that, they promised that after the war Italy could annex significant Austro-Hungarian areas in the northern Adriatic and along the Dalmatian coast which contained large areas populated by South Slavs.

In order for the Allies to fulfill their promise to Italy, they had to convince the South Slavs to give up their promise to liberate all Croats, Slovenes, and Serbs. This required, first of all, getting the Serbs to change their war aim. The Allies, in effect, promised the Serbs a Great Serbia. They could have all of Bosnia-Hercegovina, large parts of Dalmatia, and some areas populated mainly by Croats. Montenegro was promised parts of Dalmatia. But Serbian Prime Minister Pašić was adamant. He insisted on being faithful to his government's pledge of working for the liberation of all Serbs, Croats, and Slovenes.

In subsequent wartime negotiations between the Serbian government and the Yugoslav Committee (made up mainly of Slovenes, Croats, and Serbs from the South Slav areas of Austria-Hungary), an agreement was reached in July 1917 on the creation of the common state to be known as the Kingdom of the Serbs, Croats, and Slovenes. Because the meetings took place on the Greek island of Corfu, the agreement came to be called the Corfu Declaration.

Full of sentiments of unity, brotherhood, and common interests, the agreement contained fourteen specific points dealing with the organization of the future state. It was to be a "constitutional, democratic, and parliamentary monarchy with the Karadjordjević [Serbian] dynasty at the head." The final point of the declaration stated that a constituent assembly would adopt a constitution "by a numerically qualified majority," a somewhat vague and imprecise provision that was nowhere defined.

Aside from the dynasty, Serbia did not ask for any privileged status or veto power, a stance quite different from, for example, the actions of Prussia when it was uniting Germany. Serbia gave up its democratic constitution, convinced that a constituent assembly would produce a democratic one for the new state. In addition, Serbia yielded its flag, coat of arms, and other national symbols. Ante Trumbić, a Croat who represented the Yugoslav Committee at Corfu, paid high praise to Serbia: "As a state she has made the greatest sacrifice for the union of our three-named people."

While the Allies had a high regard for Serbia's brave stand against Austria-Hungary, they realized that the creation of a South Slav state would make it impossible for them to fulfill their promises to Italy. Consequently, they treated the Corfu Declaration with studied coolness. As compensation, as indicated, they assured Pašić that they were willing to see the establishment of a Great Serbia. But to Pašić that would be a betrayal of the Croats and Slovenes, as well as other Serbs.

Serbia's hope for a realization of its goals were severely weakened in 1917 when Russia, Serbia's special patron, was knocked out of the war by the Bolshevik revolution. In addition, several Allied proclamations in early 1918 gave little comfort to Serbia. In these pronouncements, Britain, France, and their new ally, the United States, mentioned the rights and aspiration of the Poles, Czechs, and others, but made no reference to the declared aspirations of the South Slavs.

When Pašić's query as to whether the omission was accidentally or intentionally "leaked," he came under attack from British pro-Yugoslav publicists and members of the Yugoslav Committee who feared he was ready to accept the Allies' offer of creating a Great Serbia. They charged him with abandoning the Yugoslav idea. Denying the charges, he issued statements in October 1918 to the British press in which he declared that the "Serbian people cannot wish a dominant role in the future kingdom," but that it was Serbia's duty to liberate all the Serbs, Croats, and Slovenes. After that they would be free to join Serbia or "create small states as in the distant past." This was not good news for the members of the Yugoslav Committee, because the South Slavs they purported to represent might continue to live under foreign rule.

By this time, South Slav politicians were being overtaken by events. In November 1918, an overwhelming number of districts in Vojvodina and Bosnia-Hercegovina decided in favor of uniting with Serbia, as did the Large National Assembly in Montenegro. Most critical for the Croats and Slovenes was the occupation of key areas of the northern Adriatic by

Italian troops seeking to assure to Italy the promises of the Treaty of London.

In light of these developments, delegates of the National Council, acting for the recently proclaimed state of Slovenes, Croats, and Serbs in Zagreb, rushed to liberated Belgrade and proposed that provisional authorities be established under Prince Alexander, pending the writing of a constitution for the new state. In their audience with Alexander, they made the following points: sovereign authority shall be exercised by Alexander; pending convocation of the constituent assembly, an agreement shall be reached on the establishment of a responsible cabinet and a temporary parliament; during the transitional period, each unit shall retain its existing authority, although under the control of the cabinet; and the constituent assembly shall be elected on the basis of direct, universal, equal, and proportional suffrage.

On December 1, 1918, Alexander accepted their statement and proclaimed the creation of the Kingdom of the Serbs, Croats, and Slovenes.

It is of more than passing interest that the Croats and Slovenes were able to leave as citizens of the Austro-Hungarian Empire and be accepted with equal rights as citizens of a victorious Kingdom of the Serbs, Croats, and Slovenes. Croatian and Slovenian soldiers and officers who had fought for Austria-Hungary were even accepted into the army of the new Yugoslav state.

At Versailles, the actions of the South Slavs in establishing the new kingdom were, in effect, ratified, and this occurred in no small measure by virtue of President Wilson's assertion that he had not heard of the Treaty of London and would not be bound by it. In Lloyd George's memoirs of the peace conference, he referred to Pašić as one of the "craftiest and most tenacious statesmen of Southeastern Europe.... The foundation of the Yugoslav Kingdom was largely his doing.... He took care that this extended realm was an accomplished fact before the Peace Conference had time to approach the problem of adjusting boundaries."[1]

The United States was the first great power to recognize the new state, in February 1919.

---

[1] *Memoirs of the Peace Conference* (New Haven, 1939), Vol. II, p. 525.

The New State

The newly created state faced unbelievable hurdles. The Serbs, Croats, and Slovenes, as well as Italian, Hungarian, Albanian and other minorities, were together in a new political entity. Serbia had a great deal of experience in democratic government, but other parts of the state had precious little or none.

The tone and style of rule in day-to-day administrative and political matters in the first year was set by the first minister of interior, Svetozar Pribićević, a Serb member of the Croat-Serb coalition in the former Zagreb Diet, a local government council allowed by the Hungarian authorities. He issued administrative regulations and appointed and dismissed local officials. As a former political co-worker with Croats, he claimed to know them well and was confident he could work with them. Some of his work, however, was resented by the Croats.

Because the citizens had lived under different legal and other systems, a special ministry was appointed, given the task of bringing equalization of the laws and a modicum of legal uniformity. But progress was painfully slow.

Economically, the new kingdom was predominantly peasant. Serbia was a land of small landholdings, while in parts of Croatia and Slovenia there were some large estates. Serbia and Montenegro were devastated by the war and had almost no industry. Croatia and Slovenia, as parts of the Habsburg domain, had a modest industrial base. While the new state was founded on a private enterprise economy, the bulk of the working capital was centered in Zagreb, with the result that investments in industry flowed toward Croatia and Slovenia. The inequality of the various regions provided for political conflicts.

Corruption, broadly defined, was another issue in the early days of the First Yugoslavia. It had its origin in wartime profiteering in the south regions of Austria-Hungary and in the immediate postwar days of the new union. Much of the alleged corruption involved conflicts of interest of government officials and legislators giving inside information to friends interested in government procurements. There were laws and administrative rules designed to eliminate corruption, but in practice they were less than effective.

Taxation was another problem. A February 1928 law concerning direct taxes equalized such taxes throughout the state, as well as increasing direct taxes as a source of government revenue. Some concessions were given to the peasants. However, the value-added tax, especially on sugar, coffee, beer, and other items, was a heavy burden on low-income citizens. Other sources of government revenue were state monopolies on such items as salt, petroleum, matches, and tobacco.

Generally speaking, economic problems did not stand in the way as a major factor in efforts to build a political consensus in the pre-1929 period, certainly less so than in the 1930s. Further comments will be found in a subsequent chapter.

Creating political institutions for the new state was difficult. The provisional parliament labored for two years, with several cabinets, and scare results. Finally, in 1921 a constituent assembly was elected. Unfortunately, the political leaders who had represented Croatia in the provisional parliament were soundly defeated by the Croatian Peasant Party, led by Stepan Radić. Radić, who had opposed the rush to Belgrade to consummate the union on December 1, 1918, decided to boycott the constituent assembly. This act denied the Croats a role in the making of the constitution for the new state. While the assembly was in session, Radić changed the name of his party to the Croatian Republican Peasant Party, and openly campaigned for an independent Croatia.

Although Croatia gave the cabinet its most serious headaches, there were problems of a general nature throughout the country. Initially, aspirations and expectations among the people were high. Recovery, however, proved slow, the effect of the war continued, efforts to establish a workable administrative system were halting, and speculators were seen to be prospering in the midst of human misery. In these circumstances, disappointment and dissatisfaction took root as well-intentioned politicians fell far short of accomplishing what was needed.

Nevertheless, a constitution was adopted in June 1921, under the leadership of Nikola Pašić, the Serbian Radical party leader. The Croats immediately condemned the constitution because, they said, it was not adopted by the required majority specified in the Corfu Declaration. That Declaration had asserted that the constitution must be adopted by a "numerically qualified majority," a vague and somewhat imprecise provision that was nowhere defined. The constituent assembly, when it met in 1921, concluded that an absolute majority of its delegates was sufficient to meet the language of Corfu. Pašić had been able to get the support of the Muslim party from Bosnia and some other small parties to achieve that majority. The Communists elected delegates, who were not allowed to take seats because the party was banned in 1921 for terrorist acts. They issued statements that they were opposed to the constitution, and argued that the *real* constitution would be written with "blood in the streets."

The new constitution provided for a parliamentary government. It was to be a unitary state with a strong central government and limited powers given to local governments. Radić, however, refused to have his party's deputies take their seats in the national parliament.

Radić, although not a peasant himself, knew the Croatian peasantry and managed to identify with it. He was adept at articulating its aspirations, aggregating its discontents, and harnessing its national consciousness to his political wagon. Contrary to the statements of some scholars in the West, he did not favor a federated Yugoslavia in which Serbia would participate. This is evident from his private correspondence and his public espousal of a Croatian republic. He sent messages to President Wilson and the heads of other states, asking for help in the realization and recognition of a Croatian republic. He wrote letters and pamphlets in an effort to enlist the support of the foreign press.

Initially, Radić was not taken too seriously, but subsequently was imprisoned for a year. While there he wrote a new Habsburg hymn for what he envisioned a new country with more than a hundred million people, all Roman Catholic. In 1925, however, he accepted the constitution, the monarchy, and the political order, and even dropped the word "republican" from his party's name.

At the same time, Radić's party joined a political coalition headed by Nikola Pašić, who had been prime minister since early 1921. Within a brief period, Radić went from being a prisoner in the dock to a minister in the cabinet.

Apparently, Radić had been ready to reach an agreement a year earlier when he told some of his supporters that he was willing to recognize the monarchy, but he had added: "For God's sake, give me time to turn my automobile around.... I cannot change all of my politics at once."[2]

But Serbs were also divided, especially after the formation of a new political party, the Democratic Party, as a competitor of the Serbian Radical Party which had commanded strong support among Serbs before the First World War. Radical Party strength was almost exclusively in Serbia, while Democrats sought support throughout the new state. This added to the already existing situation—no one political party could get a majority in parliament. Hence all cabinets had to be coalition cabinets, guaranteeing political instability.

The high hopes stemming from the Pašić-Radić agreement turned sour. Pašić left his post as prime minister in April 1926 and died in December. The new cabinet of the Radicals plus Radić soon entered stormy waters. Radić and his party colleagues increasingly engaged in obstructionist tactics in parliament. In the difficult days of early 1928, a Radical deputy from Montenegro shot Radić and several of his colleagues during a parliamentary session. Two died almost immediately, but Radić recovered, only to die in August of secondary infections from his diabetes. The Croatian deputies and their political associates left parliament.

For a time, King Alexander made several efforts to find a political solution, including making the leader of the Slovene People's Party, Anton Korošec, prime minister. In January 1929, however, the king took personal power, convinced that the system of parliamentary democracy had failed to create a consensus. Declaring his move would be temporary, he ruled mainly through non-political ministers, seeking to impose consensus from above. He changed the name of the country to Yugoslavia and divided it into nine administrative regions, called *banovinas*, after a Croatian term meaning governor, in an effort to eliminate narrow historical entities. This was in accord with his earlier pro-Yugoslav orientation of giving his three sons Serbian, Croatian, and Slovenian first names.

In 1931, Alexander modified his rule by presenting the country with a new constitution. His aim was to reestablish democracy in a somewhat

---

2 Dragoljub Jovanović, *Ljudi, Ljudi...* (Belgrade, 1973), vol. I, p. 326.

limited form that came to be called "guided democracy" in the period after the Second World War.

In foreign affairs he was instrumental in the creation of the Little Entente (Yugoslavia, Romania, and Czechoslovakia) in close collaboration with France. It was while on an official visit to France in October 1934 that he and the French foreign minister were assassinated by members of the Internal Macedonian Revolutionary Organization (IMRO) in a well-organized plot coordinated between the Croatian extremist movement know as Ustaše, which was led by Ante Pavelić, who had fled to Italy in the early years of the king's personal rule.

Governing Without Alexander

Because his eldest son, Peter, was only eleven years old, royal powers were assumed by a regency of three men, as provided in the king's will. Prince Paul, Alexander's first cousin, in effect soon became the regency. He confided to a close associate of the king that he had not been nurtured for the role, that politics had never interested him, that Alexander never instructed him in anything. Thus he found himself in a delicate position, in terms of both domestic and foreign affairs. Nevertheless, he soon demonstrated a determination to bring about change.

Before tackling Prince Paul's major achievement—the agreement with the Croats—it is necessary to deal with a church problem.

The State and the Church

As indicated elsewhere, the Serbs are Serbian Orthodox, while the Croats and Slovenes are Roman Catholic. And a large minority are Muslims. The religious differences, however, did not produce discord. But in 1937, the broad masses were moved, especially in Serbia, over the ratification of a concordat with the Vatican. The matter was inherited by the prime minister Milan Stojadinović cabinet.

The concordat was largely King Alexander's doing. When the Yugoslav state was formed in 1918, several concordats with the Vatican were in existence. Prime Minister Pašić recognized the need to clarify this situation and in 1924 appointed a committee to study the matter. Since no resolution of the problem had been reached by 1929, Alexander took it upon himself personally to handle the matter. To that end he engaged the leading expert on concordats, Professor Charles Loiseau of France, to assist him. Subsequently he sent a Roman Catholic priest to Rome for direct negotiations. The resulting draft received the enthusiastic approval of Professor Loiseau.

Alexander's untimely death interrupted the process. Nevertheless, the Jeftić cabinet concluded the arrangements for the signing on July 15, 1935. When Stojadinović replaced Jeftić, he decided not to change that date. Before sending his minister of justice, Croat Catholic Ljudevit Auer, to sign the document in Rome, Stojadinović asked Auer to inform Patriarch Varnava of the Serbian Orthodox Church, who gave his blessing. Although Varnava had a copy of the document, it seems that he gave his blessing mainly on the basis of personal assurances he had received from Prince Paul and other leading political figures rather than any careful reading of the document. Once the Patriarch and his close associates had read the fine print, however, they became convinced that the concordat gave the Roman Catholic Church privileges that other religious bodies did not have, yet neither they nor the Serbian Church had done nothing in over a year.

Why then did the concordat become an apple of discord when Stojadinović brought it for ratification by the Skupština? The best answer is that his opponents believed that it could be exploited for partisan political purposes. They distributed distorted versions of the concordat and circulated pamphlets asserting that the Catholic Church would use its new privileges to proselyte in Orthodox areas. And the Orthodox Church took strong stands against the concordat, threatening excommunication of Orthodox cabinet members as well as Orthodox deputies who voted for the concordat.

When it became evident that Stojadinović intended to carry through with his plans, Patriarch Varnava called the Assembly of Bishops into session on May 26, 1937. The assembly again criticized politicians who were seeking to exploit a religious question for other purposes, but it found the concordat injurious to the vital interests of the Serbian Orthodox Church. The press did not play an objective role. It was not easy to determine the truth. Seemingly, neither Stojadinović nor Prince Paul appreciated the seriousness of the situation.

While the discussions were in progress in the Skupština, Patriarch Varnava took seriously ill. To make matters worse, he died on the very day that the concordat was to be ratified, amid unfounded rumors that he had been poisoned. Although ratified unaltered by a comfortable majority, the concordat was not submitted to the Senate. In Stojadinović's words, he decided to return it to the desk drawer where he had found it. It never went into effect during the existence of the First Yugoslavia.

The Agreement with the Croats: Sporazum

The principal achievement of Paul's relatively brief rule was an agreement (a *sporazum*) with the Croatian leader, Vladko Maček, providing for a Croatian geographic unit with considerable autonomy. It was signed on August 20, 1939, on the eve of the Second World War. A variety of complex factors led to the accord. Immediate events were ominous, among them the dismemberment of Czechoslovakia by Hitler after the Munich Pact and Hitler's exploitation of separatist tendencies in Slovakia (which later became a puppet regime under Catholic priest Father Josef Tiso). Maček had publicly and privately used the threat of secession and foreign backing, including negotiations with Italian dictator Mussolini, effectively to speed up the changes he wanted.

Maček kept demanding a constituent assembly that would write a new constitution, but Paul and his constitutional advisers insisted that changing the constitution was illegal while King Peter was a minor. In the end they found a legal and constitutional basis for allowing concession to the Croats without formally altering the constitution. Article 116 provided that in exceptional circumstances such as war, mobilization, disturbance, or rebellion, when the security of the state or the public interest was endangered, the king could "temporarily take by decree all extraordinary and necessary measures, independently of constitutional or legal provisions, in the whole kingdom or in one part." The only limiting provision was that such measures must subsequently be submitted to parliament for confirmation, which incidentally was never done.

The sporazum created a large geographic unit known as the Banovina of Croatia, which included the territory mainly and traditionally inhabited by Croatians, as well as most of Slavonia (mixed Serb and Croat), Dalmatia (mainly Croatian with a sizeable Orthodox population), and parts of Bosnia-Hercegovina (Croats, Serbs, and Muslims). The definitive boundaries were to be determined at the time of the reorganization of the state. Approximately one-fourth of the new banovina's population of four and a half million was Serb.

The Banovina of Croatia was to have its own popularly elected parliament and a governor appointed by the king. To a significant degree, therefore, the 1931 constitution was amended. Unitarism was not formally abolished, but the autonomy of the Banovina of Croatia was tantamount to liquidation of it.

Considerable power, including fiscal, was to be delegated to the banovina authorities, though there would be some overlapping. The central government would continue to have control over foreign affairs, defense, communication, and transport. A constitutional court was to be created to decide cases of conflict in jurisdiction. Many things were left undecided; some were not done for several months. As an example, no electoral law was passed, so there were no elections either nationally or for the Croatian parliament, and no constitutional court was established.

A royal decree, published as part of the agreement, declared that provisions concerning the Banovina of Croatia could be extended to other banovinas, including the amalgamation of territories or other alterations of boundaries. Presumably, this would guarantee that Serbian and Slovenian units could be established. To that end, commissions were actually set up to draft decrees creating Serbian and Slovene units, but the outbreak of World War II prevented further action.

It is difficult to summarize the various reactions to the sporazum. Experts were sharply divided on its constitutionality. Since the cabinet continually postponed the election of a new national parliament, the agreement never received the ultimate constitutional sanction. Some viewed the agreement as creating a state within a state. Certainly, a large majority of Serbs believed that they would not be masters in their own house. Feeling that the Croats had obtained rights still denied to Serbs, they felt forced to demand the creation of a Serbian unit, but the coming war put an end to their dreams.

The reaction of the political parties was mixed. Those who had in the past collaborated with Maček felt betrayed, although they did not always show it immediately. Others were cautious, worried that the agreement would undermine the unity of the state. Some, including the Yugoslav Muslim Organization and the Slovene People's Party, were divided. Older Radicals were disinclined to demand a Serbian unit because this would signify acceptance of federalism. The Democrats, who had earlier accepted the principle of federalism, began pointedly emphasizing the Serb population of Bosnia-Hercegovina (almost half) and Macedonia (about two-thirds).

The Croats, not denying the justice of Serbian and other demands for a reorganization of the state, felt that this should come only after the election of a new parliament that would ratify the sporazum. They feared that the establishment of Slovene and Serbian banovinas, especially the latter, might preclude them from realizing their anticipated additional demands. This attitude created ill will outside Croatia where the general view was that Croatia had already been given too much territory.

Not long after the 1939 agreement was signed, two contradictory documents depicted the Croatian attitude toward the sporazum. In a circular to party offices, dated October 10, 1939, the Croatian Peasant Party leadership expressed complete satisfaction with the way in which the Yugoslav government was implementing the agreement. It did criticize the uncooperative attitude of the bureaucracy inside the Banovina. Viewing the agreement as the first phase in the total reconstruction of the state, it said that this was a calculated way of blunting separatist propaganda attacking Maček for betraying the idea of an independent Croatian state.

The other document, circulated at the same time, spoke completely contrary to the official one. It was labeled strictly confidential, but did not carry Maček's name or the party seal. Many were convinced that it had originated with the leadership, and some were sure that Maček had approved it. It asserted that in signing the sporazum the Croatian Peasant Party had not given up the idea of an independent Croatia. Rather it was the first step toward its creation. Moreover, the agreement had achieved two goals: it had destroyed the integrity of the state—and consequently "Yugoslavia" should never be used, but simply "state union"; and the national government had been forced to move away from the idea of national unity, thereby destroying the foundations of Yugoslavia. Additional instructions told party members that in the central government they should always speak of "Croatian ministers" and the Banovina of Croatia should always be referred to simply as Croatia; Croats should always speak of a free and independent Croatia and of Croatian interests. Party members in the banovina were receiving similar directives "from Zagreb." From the autumn of 1939, many party organizations and local members followed the secret circular's instructions.

Some Croats maintained that the secret circular did not originate with party sources and therefore was not authentic. After World War II, however, a Yugoslav historian, Veselin Djuretić, who conducted research in the Soviet Union, reported that on the basis of authoritative Soviet sources it was irrefutable that the prewar Croatian Peasant Party's divisive anti-Serbian and anti-Yugoslav circular was not a forgery, but an original.[3]

The End of the First Yugoslavia

The sporazum had been signed in August: World War II broke out in September. Poland was soon defeated, and Belgium, Holland, and France fell in the spring of 1940. At that point, for Yugoslavia all alternatives were unpromising. The rapid fall of France was a severe blow. The British were in no position to offer assistance, yet they expected the Yugoslav government and its army to rebuff Nazi pressure to adhere to the Tripartite Pact of Germany, Italy, and Japan. Croat and Slovene leaders were resolutely in favor of signing the pact. The Serbs, including Prime Minister Dragiša Cvetković, were unswervingly opposed. Then in January 1941, British Prime Minister Winston Churchill told Prince Paul that neutrality was not enough. Cvetković and Paul still believed that to enter the war meant committing national suicide. Their one hope was to gain delays so that Hitler might leave them alone.

As it turned out, despite Hitler's impatience, the Yugoslav leaders proved to be tough negotiators. Before signing anything with the Axis, they asked for concessions, which earlier Balkan signers had not. Hitler declared that what he was proposing to Yugoslavia was not in fact the

---

3 Veselin Djuretić, *Demolition of the Serbs in the 20th Century: Background of the Current Drama in Dismembered Yugoslavia* (Skokie, IL: Great Lakes Graphics, Inc., 1994), pp. 67-79.

Tripartite Pact. In a personal meeting with Paul, he took the same line, but also offered concrete guarantees.

The Yugoslavs signed a pact on March 25, 1941. At that time, Cvetković got three brief notes signed by the German foreign minister. The first promised that "for all time" Germany would "respect the sovereignty of Yugoslavia." The second promised that the Axis powers would "not during the war demand of Yugoslavia the passage or transport of military forces through Yugoslav territory." The third stated that Italy and Germany would not ask Yugoslavia for any military assistance, leaving open the possibility that Yugoslavia might at some point find it in its interest to offer help. Hitler agreed that the Yugoslavs could publish the first and third notes, but not the second.

The ink was hardly dry on the documents when, on the night of March 26–27, a military coup overthrew the Cvetković-Maček cabinet. The coup leaders declared young King Peter of age and ousted Prince Paul as regent. The new Prime Minister, General Dušan Simović, declared that the new cabinet would abide by all international agreements that Yugoslavia had signed. When noted Yugoslav scholar Slobodan Jovanović, a vice-premier in Simović's cabinet, examined the agreement signed with Germany, he asserted: "There is nothing here that could not be accepted." Yet the Cvetković-Maček cabinet was overthrown allegedly because of unwarranted concessions to Germany.

But Hitler was not amused; he ordered a massive attack, which ended the life of the First Yugoslavia.

Consequently, there was no way of knowing if the sporazum was ever a possible first step in the establishment of a viable political system in the First Yugoslavia.

J. B. Hoptner, an American scholar who studied the March 1941 coup, concluded that the Allied leaders "failed to extend to Yugoslavia the patience and diplomatic restraint they showed to Sweden—despite the fact that Sweden, under conditions similar to those facing Yugoslavia, signed an agreement with Germany permitting a steady flow of German military traffic to pass over its borders."[4] A subsequent study in

---

[4] *Yugoslavia in Crisis, 1934–1941* (New York: Columbia University Press, 1962), pp. 298-9.

Italy confirmed the judgment reached by Hoptner: the coup was in the interests of Britain and, as it turned out, of the Soviet Union, but suicidal for Yugoslavia, as Prince Paul and Cvetković had foreseen.

XI

Serbia in the Second Yugoslavia

The German-Italian attack on Yugoslavia in April 1941 was, for Serbia, the beginning of a long downhill slide toward catastrophe. First was military defeat and destruction of the Yugoslav state. Simultaneously was the creation of the Axis satellite Croatian state, the so-called Independent State of Croatia, under the leadership of Ante Pavelić. Then came the struggle between two guerrilla movements—a civil war that led to the establishment of the Second Yugoslavia, or Communist Yugoslavia. The ultimate failure of that state, the precursor of new civil wars, was for Serbia the end of the long trail of tears, a dreaded end and a new beginning.

Resistance to the Axis military attack collapsed within two weeks. Yugoslavia was torn apart. The pro-Axis Croatian state, in addition to Croatian areas, got all of Bosnia-Hercegovina and some other Serbian areas. Slovenia was absorbed by Germany. Other parts of Yugoslavia were ceded to Italy, Hungary, and Bulgaria. The remainder of the state was divided into two occupation zones: one was German, composed mainly of Serbia under the civil administration of Serbian General Milan Nedić (who performed a role similar to that of General Petain in France), and the other Italian, centered in Montenegro and areas northward, especially parts of Dalmatia not already consigned to annexation by Italy.

The satellite Croatian state, ruled by Ante Pavelić, the head of the so-called Ustashe movement, was organized and functioned much like Mussolini's Fascist regime. He and his cohorts came with the Italian troops. He was forced to swallow a bitter pill: the beautiful coastal area of Dalmatia, the pride of all Croats, was annexed by Italy. In addition, Pavelić was forced to accept as head of state Italy's Duke of Spoleto, but this was pro forma only because the Duke never appeared in Zagreb to assume his throne.

Following Hitler's attack on the Soviet Union in June 1941, Pavelić declared war and sent a division to fight alongside the Nazis on the Eastern front. After the Japanese attack on Pearl Harbor, Pavelić also declared war on the United States and Great Britain.

At home, Pavelić promulgated decrees to deal with opponents, real or imagined. Under them a large number of Serbs, as well as Jews and Gypsies, were massacred or driven from Croatia. Croat propagandists are still forced to dissemble or to quibble over the size of their massacre. The estimates of the number of Serbs killed vary from 300,000 to more than a million. A generally accepted figure among scholars is 500,000 to around 750,000. Even German officials in Croatia were horrified by the nature and extent of the killings, and protested to their Croatian associates, but their protests seem to have fallen on deaf ears.

In Serbia the people also suffered, but the suffering there was of a different order. Not long after the Nazi occupation began, some troops fled to the hills rather than surrender to the Germans. They began as a group under the command of General Draža Mihailović, and came to be known as the Yugoslav Army in the Homeland, but more popularly as the Chetniks. They engaged in some anti-German actions which brought severe retributions—50 Serbian hostages for every German soldier killed, 100 hostages for every officer killed. Mihailović soon realized that actions against the Germans were suicidal, and was forced to stop or limit them.

Initially, the Chetniks had no political aims other than to assist the Allies in defeating the Axis powers. But when the Nazis attacked the Soviet Union, and the Yugoslav Communists organized a competing guerrilla movement, Mihailović worked out a liberal democratic program and declared that the Yugoslav peoples should be allowed to determine their own political future once they were free to do so.

The Yugoslav Communists took action against the Germans only after the attack on the Soviet Union. Then under the leadership of Josip Broz, later better known as Tito, they sought to portray their National Liberation Movement, popularly known as Partisans, as broad and allegedly liberally democratic. Knowing that they had little following among the people, they concealed their real aims and hid the fact that they were Communists. They hoped that by disguising their ultimate objectives, and with the help of the Soviets, they would be successful in gaining power. Once in power, they did not hesitate to talk of their tactics and successes.

The essential difference between the Chetniks and the Partisans was in their aims. The former pursued a national struggle for liberation from the occupier, the latter was primarily interested in seizing power. Mihailović believed in the freedom of choice for the Yugoslav peoples; Tito in a dictatorship of the proletariat. In the fall of 1941, Tito and Mihailović met to discuss a common front against the Nazis, but given the basic difference in aims it was unrealistic to hope for a united front, and the two men parted as bitter enemies. The tragedy of the brutal struggles between them that followed was the more poignant because most of the recruits on both sides were Serbs. The Montenegrin Serbs suffered especially by being split between the two forces.

Mihailović succeeded in driving the Partisans out of Serbia when he realized what their real objectives were. They retreated mainly to the Montenegrin Mountains in territory under Italian control. Some went into hiding in the fascist Croatian state, where they found abundant recruits among the Serbs who had fled from the Ustashe massacres. The Partisans never returned to Serbia in significant numbers until Soviet troops arrived at the Danube in late 1944.

In mid-1942, charges were heard from the Tito camp that Mihailović was collaborating with the Germans and Italians. These charges were untrue, although there were instances where certain Chetniks turned to Italian troops for protection from the Croatian Ustashe bloodthirsty elements. Nevertheless, these charges in the long run aided the Partisans. As a matter of fact, both Chetniks and Partisans were anti-Axis. As indicated above, Mihailović concluded that the merciless Nazi vengeance against the Serb population in areas where his men took actions against the Germans steered him to caution. The Communist-led Partisans, on the other hand, were not concerned with reprisals, seeing in them causes for recruitment to their ranks. Admissions of this was to be found in postwar Partisan publications.

The British took the lead in dealing with the Yugoslav resistance movements. While aware that both movements were anti-Nazi, the British believed reports from their agents that the Partisans were doing more guerrilla fighting, and therefore sent more assistance to them. It is now known that reports of liaison officers, sent through British intelligence in Cairo, were being handled by a member of the British Communist Party, who passed on to London those favorable to the Partisans and withheld those favorable to Mihailović. Significant actions of the Chetniks against the enemy were often reported as actions of the Partisans.

In any case, Churchill changed Allied policy toward Yugoslavia in September 1943. British aid, which had been flowing generously to Tito, was increased and that to Mihailović, which had never been much, was cut off. Some raised questions about the change, especially in the United States. It should be noted that President Franklin Roosevelt had once questioned whether Yugoslavia should be reconstituted. He noted that "Croats and Serbs had nothing in common, and that it was ridiculous to try to force such antagonistic peoples to live together." He thought that Serbia should be established as a separate nation and Croatia should be put under trusteeship. But the policy change moved on. Churchill had no doubts. Even when his trusted adviser Fitzroy Maclean told him in Cairo (on his way home from the Teheran conference) that eventually the Partisans would win and that after the war they would establish a Communist system in Yugoslavia. Churchill's response was to ask Maclean if he planned to live in Yugoslavia after the war. When Maclean answered no, Churchill said: "Neither do I, so the less that you and I worry about the type of political system that the Yugoslavs will have after the war, the better."

At that time, the Partisans were entrenched mainly in the mountains of Montenegro and Bosnia-Hercegovina. There were almost none in Croatia, and very few in Serbia, where they appeared in numbers only after the Red Army crossed into Yugoslavia. Ironically, it was the Chetniks who first welcomed the Soviet troops, but the Soviets and Partisans liquidated them.

The Partisans were also helped by the Italian surrender. Mihailović had seized sizeable war materiel. The Italian Venezia division surrendered to the Chetniks, but they were not allowed to get its large cache of arms because, for some still unexplained reason, the head of the British military mission prevented it. Moreover, under the terms of the armistice, Italian commanders were obliged to surrender to Tito's forces.

Establishing a Communist System

The end of the war found Tito's Communist forces in Belgrade, in large part courtesy of the Soviet Red Army. Tito's regime quickly got recognition from Allied and other countries. It then proceeded to establish a Communist system, following closely the Soviet pattern, after going through the motions of manipulated elections and other actions that included non-Communist parties which Tito had promised to the Western powers. Not only were the non-Communist parties pushed aside, but those that had joined the Communists as allies were ousted as soon as they uttered policy statements that were independent of the regime's position. The best examples were Dragoljub Jovanović's left Agrarians. Jovanović was even arrested and imprisoned for nearly 10 years. That constituted an inglorious end to the promise that non-Communists had a place in Tito's regime.

Yugoslavia was divided into six republics, ostensibly along nationality lines: Slovenia, Croatia, Serbia, Montenegro, Macedonia, Bosnia-Hercegovina. The last was created in part because of a complex Serb, Croat, Muslim population combination and in part to avoid a Serb-Croat struggle for control. And Tito wanted to prevent Bosnian Serbs from becoming part of Serbia. The regime's creation of a separate Muslim ethnic group there did not take place until the late 1960s. And inside Serbia were created two autonomous provinces: Kosovo with a large Albanian population, some alleged a majority; and Vojvodina, with a large Hungarian minority. The establishment of these provinces would lessen the strength of the Serbs. These anti-Serb moves were motivated in part because Tito's Partisans had had little support in Serbia, which was the heart of Mihailović's movement.

Tito's territorial organization of Yugoslavia left 40 percent of the Serbs in units outside Serbia proper. The boundaries were rather arbitrary and were to cause no end of trouble when certain republics sought to secede in 1991.

The structure of Tito's government was based on a constitution virtually the same as that of the Soviet Union. The Communists prided themselves in calling it the "Dictatorship of the Proletariat." This meant that the Communist Party had a monopoly of power. After an initial period, when some parties were allied with the Communists, no other party or political movement was allowed to exist.

The so-called federal system was only a front. The individual republics had no powers independent of the central government.

The Harnessing of the Masses to the Dictatorship

Communist dictatorships have perfected a variety of elaborate techniques for regimenting the masses. It is no exaggeration to say that these are both more intensive and more extensive than those developed by any other despotism known to man. Like other totalitarian governments, Tito's Yugoslav regime brooked no opposition and tolerated no passivity. In its determination to obliterate opposition and to harness the people to do its bidding, the regime left no stone unturned. I have chosen to call this whole process "harnessing the masses to the dictatorship." It is guided by the Agitation and Propaganda (*Agitprop*) section of the Party's Central Committee. I believe that I am the first American political scientist to have embraced this comprehensive approach. The description covers nearly 70 pages in my *Tito's Promised Land: Yugoslavia*. Obviously, my treatment here must be much briefer.

*   *   *

Unlike revolutions of past centuries, modern-day Communism uprisings are characterized by a more systematic, and cold-blooded ruthlessness, and an all-encompassing surveillance of the people within the domain of its power. The regime's system can be divided into three broad or general categories: (1) force and fear, (2) monopolizing public opinion, (3) extensive mobilizing of the organizational life of the society.

The Yugoslav Communists were busy preparing lists of enemies even before they came to power. Once in power the Titoists liquidated thousands of those they judged enemies. There was scarcely a city or town where a number of leading citizens (usually doctors, lawyers, judges, teachers, merchants, journalists, and writers) were not summarily liquidated, many of them without benefit of judicial process. Those considered somewhat less dangerous were sent off to prisons.

Serbia probably was the hardest hit by the secret police, for the Serbs had not only supported Tito's guerrilla opponent, Mihailović, but in addition, had a history of recorded violence toward tyrannical rulers. The fact that the regime was less harsh in some other regions, however, did not make it likeable.

Communist terror was also visited upon young people. This was especially true in Belgrade where the Communist leaders did not like the opposition to the regime which they claimed they found among young people.

The secret police obviously could not be everywhere, hence it organized what I have called "the secret police auxiliary," a widespread web of informers. These were generally willing and unwilling, creating all sorts of uncomfortable situations, with neighbor suspecting neighbor. Sometimes these situations reached even inside families. A system of informers made trust difficult or impossible. But the regime was not above even using schoolchildren in its purposes.

* * *

Yet no Communist regime can afford to limit its control over the masses to techniques of force and fear. Public opinion is important, not in the sense of wanting to satisfy popular demands, but to gain information on how best to promote regime programs. It is not unexpected, therefore, that in attempting to get their views accepted, Communists not only strive for ownership and control of the instrumentalities of public opinion, but also to exclude competing influences to the utmost of their ability.

Although a few independent newspapers were able to begin publishing immediately after liberation, they were snuffed out or taken over by the government soon after the Communists were firmly in power. It is impossible to appreciate the government's monopoly in the field of public opinion unless one keeps in mind the fact that there were no privately owned newspaper, printing presses, or stocks of newsprint. There were no privately owned movie houses; no private producing or importing film enterprises. There were no privately owned theaters and no privately produced plays. In the later years of Yugoslav communism, some of this changed.

Yugoslav propaganda strategists did not stop with ownership and control. They stressed "quality," by which they meant that no one should be permitted to stand aside or remain aloof from political polemics. "Freedom of the press" is extended by the creation of special newspapers for all groups in the population.

No longer could poets, musicians, writers, or artists argue that theirs is a nonpolitical life. During the brief electoral campaign of 1950, for example, over twenty of the leading writers contributed from twenty to sixty lines each in two issues of the *Literary News*, all expressing their happiness and thankfulness to Tito and the Communist Party. Adding to this chorus of unanimity, a group of musicians, in another newspaper, proclaimed that a vote for the regime was "a vote for the greater blossoming of art."

*   *   *

To assist in harnessing the masses to the dictatorship, the party spewed forth a welter of organization, stemming like roots from the central branch, spreading in all directions, dividing and subdividing. Nearly all of these organizations were like parasites—economically unproductive, but all with budgets that dipped into the state treasury. They published newspapers and magazines, organized special outings, assembled for various congresses, and in general found ways to eat their way through what, for Yugoslavia at least, was fantastic sums of money.

In imitation of the Soviets, the Yugoslav Communists had from the beginning a strong penchant for mass organizations. The most notable of these was the People's Front, subsequently renamed The Socialist Alliance of Working People. Ostensibly a coalition of political parties and other groupings, at one time allegedly proving that Tito's Communist regime was "broadly representative," the People's Front turned out to be an appendage of the Communist Party whose members constituted the decisive corps of all such organizations.

Fundamentally, the mass organizations performed two types of tasks. They performed some useful physical activity in the postwar reconstruction period. More importantly, however, they served as additional vehicles by means of which the party spread the Marxian gospel and at the same time agitated for an ever-increasing effort to achieve the goals of the regime's economic plan.

*   *   *

In all their efforts to harness the masses to the regime, the Yugoslav Communists devoted more of their energies to youth than to any other segment of the population. The importance of youth to them is evidenced in party proclamations stating that the main task of young Communists under 24 years of age is to work in youth organizations and with youth, and by the constant, systematic and widespread purposive efforts of the Communist Party and its subsidiary organizations to win the allegiance of the youth.

Concretely, this meant that the party was concerned with the pre-school years, and most certainly the school years—teachers, books, and extra-curricular activities. When the Communists first came to power, they faced many problems in education—the physical destruction of schools during the civil war, the loss of teachers in the war or in flight from the country, and the killing or imprisonment of "unreliable" teachers. Perhaps most important of all, the Communists faced the enormous task of reshaping a people's mode of thought and behavior, of revising their national, cultural, and spiritual values.

*   *   *

Finally, in its task to harness the masses to the dictatorship, the party had to deal with competing influences. The most important of these were religion and the family. The regime developed several different programs to impede or minimize the activities of churches and families. For the most part, the Yugoslav Communists copied the Soviet regime. After the Tito-Stalin break in 1948, the Yugoslav leaders modified many of their programs and policies. And as the next chapter will show, differences among Communists in the various republics led to many conflicts and changes.

All of the above-described efforts of the Tito regime to shackle the masses to the dictatorship were characterized by one overriding purpose—to force everyone to surrender his independence of thought and to embrace whatever the Communist leaders offered. Once having yielded their freedom to think for themselves, the people were expected to abandon their independence of action and to accept regimentation of body as well as mind.

*   *   *

Taking Care of Party Members

The regime did not ignore the welfare of its members. Among other things, it provided special stores for party members. The most popular were the exclusive food stores which members of the diplomatic corps could also patronize. After the break with Moscow in 1948, these stores were gradually phased out. Party members demonstrated their selfishness and acquisitiveness and taste for luxury. This is well described by one-time Tito comrade Milovan Djilas in his book, *The New Class*. He observes how party members had fought in the Communist revolution, ready to give up their lives, but afterward became "characterless wretches." When asked to explain the change, he responded with: "human nature." That, of course, was a non-Marxist reply, because Marxism held that human nature was good and that selfishness in capitalism caused persons to seek selfish goals.

On the economic front, the regime also imitated the Soviet Union. It launched a movement to industrialize; in many instances projects soon ran out of materials as well as qualified personnel, leaving partially completed projects. In agriculture, the regime stressed collectivization, which met with great opposition, often followed by arrests and imprisonment. Simultaneously with collectivization, the regime instituted a system of forcing peasants to deliver set amounts of produce at ridiculously low prices. This also met with great opposition, in part because the government often asked peasants to deliver more than the peasants produced. The regime often told such peasants to buy produce from neighbors.

By 1953, the Communists realized that their agriculture policies were failures, and began to retrench by permitting peasants to leave collective farms. In many instances, the peasant could not get his land back, and was forced to accept what the government gave him. Moreover, peasants were limited to ten hectares of land, irrespective of how much they had brought in. The inauguration of some decentralization in the economy resulted in some improvement in the living standard for the average person. The permission for citizens to make some foreign trips, usually to Italy and Greece, eased what had been a tight dictatorship. Also, the permission for limited personal enterprises (e.g., small bakeries, shoe repair, etc.) came to be labeled "consumerism" which was greatly welcome. Some called these developments as at least an element of freedom. All in all, it was generally agreed that Yugoslav citizens were better off than those in any Soviet satellite, to say nothing of the Soviet Union itself.

In foreign affairs, Yugoslavia had become a most loyal satellite of the Soviet Union. But in June 1948, a break between Moscow and Belgrade erupted. There were charges and countercharges. Stalin accused Tito of abandoning the Marxist road. And Tito countered that the Yugoslavs were true to Marxist principles.

The essence of the conflict was the failure of the Yugoslavs to be subservient to Moscow's wishes. The Yugoslavs discovered that Moscow had its agents in various Yugoslav institutions, even in the Communist Party. Following Stalin's expulsion of the Yugoslav party from the Cominform, a Communist International that Moscow established with headquarters in Bucharest, the Yugoslavs revealed that two members of its top party organ, the Politburo (Sreten Žujović, a Serb, and Andrija Hebrang, a Croat), were really Stalin's agents. They were promptly dismissed. Hebrang was arrested and subsequently died in prison under strange circumstances.

What followed was a purge of the Yugoslav party of suspected Soviet sympathizers, known widely as "Cominformists." The worst elements were incarcerated on an island in the Adriatic popularly known as "Goli Otok" (naked isle). There were about 12,000 of them. The reports of beatings and other forms of mistreatment of the alleged pro-Soviet inmates were legion, but kept secret until many years later. I personally knew one of the unfortunates, whom I met soon after my arrival in Belgrade to take up my post at the American Embassy in November 1947.

He was introduced as the secretary of, at that time, the nonexistent Press Club. At our brief encounters he was quite cool.

The day after the break with Moscow was announced, however, we met by chance on the street and he was friendly and seemingly eager to talk. After that he was a source of some information about the split with Moscow. After a small dinner at our house, he and our Deputy Chief of Mission (R. Borden Reams) talked until about 4 AM, with me acting as interpreter. Some days after that he came to my office for the first time. At prior meetings he had always said, "Tito and the party are one and the same thing." This time his attitude was different. My response was: "Come on, Jovo, you are trying to provoke me." "No," he said, "I think Stalin is right."

A few days later he was arrested, and off to Goli Otok.

Some years later, after his release, we saw each other briefly at a Belgrade restaurant, and spoke, but I never had occasion to talk with him about Goli Otok. I do not know if he would have talked about his experiences there.

Subsequently, Tito decided that Yugoslavia would be in neither camp—Soviet or the West. Rather, he championed a non-aligned group of nations that would be independent of the two major camps. Among these were India, Egypt, and Cuba. In the long run some in the non-aligned camp exploited the Yugoslav connection, but the Yugoslavs did not profit much from that association. Moreover, after Stalin's death the Yugoslavs made a number of moves to repair their relations with Moscow. The disintegration of the Soviet Union, beginning in 1989, ended the era of hostile camps.

Domestically, following the break with the Soviets, the Yugoslavs began to experiment in economic policies while retaining monopoly of political power in the Communist Party (the name of the party was formally changed in 1952 to the League of Yugoslav Communists). The changes in economic policy were described as "Self-Management." Although studied, admired, and praised by various sources outside of Yugoslavia, in actual practice and in the long run, Self-Management was a failure. The biggest difficulty was the problem of conflict with Party policy, so that differences were resolved by having the Party getting its way.

Another problem was the inclination of workers councils to favor the workers at the cost of profitability of the enterprise. A further difficulty was the determination of local Party leaders to keep unprofitable local enterprises functioning. These came to be called "political factories" in popular parlance. Then there was the problem of duplication, i.e., the determination of each republic to keep enterprises afloat even when they could not compete with enterprises in other republics. Republics also competed with each other in business marketing in other countries. Still another stumbling block was the failure of certain republics to ship raw materials to other republics. The need to change locomotives at republic boundaries was another problem.

The changes in the economy, stressing decentralization, were taken advantage of by certain republics to, in essence, create an oligarchy, severely limiting trade between and among the republics. This led to political isolation and the stressing of the importance of ethnic identity. The major consequence was the weakening of loyalty to the nation, to Yugoslavia.

For the Serbs, the Second Yugoslavia was not a good experience. The Serbs were made to feel that they were the ones who were guilty for all the things that went wrong in the First Yugoslavia, and were now paying for their sins. There was a lot of hard work for them but little in the way of rewards. They were scattered among several geographic units. They were forced to accept autonomy for Vojvodina and Kosovo. The latter, the cradle of the Serbian nation, was torn, so to speak, from its body. Moreover, they were forced into an economic system—collectivization—that they did not want. They had long been dedicated to private enterprise and individualism. In short, they believed in the values that their fathers and mothers had taught them. And now they were living in a society whose values were foreign to those that had characterized the Serbian way of life for generations.

XII

Serbia and the Disintegration of Yugoslavia

The above chapters constitute a thumbnail sketch of Serbia's long history. As other peoples in ancient times, the Serbs had family and tribal loyalties, and some of these resulted in conflicts and struggles for power. In Serbian lands, success was achieved by the Nemanjić family with the beginnings of the medieval Serbian state. As Chapter One has demonstrated, this was a talented family with strong Christian leanings.

The success of the Nemanjićes is testified to by the fact that for over one hundred years medieval Serbia was the strongest state in the Balkans. The most visible symbols of that Serbian heritage are Tsar Dušan's Code of Laws and the many Serbian Orthodox Church monasteries, some of which have been selected by international art experts as world treasures. Most of these monasteries are in Kosovo, the cradle of the Serbian nation, and in recent years the targets of Kosovo demolition squads.

Moreover, medieval Serbia was part of the international community, relating on a state-to-state basis in matters of political, military, and cultural affairs. Serbian royal courts communicated on levels of respect and honor with Venetian Doges, Hungarian kings, Bulgarian tsars, and Byzantine emperors.

In 1389, however, Serbian forces met defeat at Kosovo by the Ottoman Turks, and thus began the dissolution of the Serbian state and the inauguration of over 400 years of foreign rule over the Serbs. The great wonder is that during those long years the Serbs were able to retain a sense of national identity and a notion of physical heritage. Most historians are convinced that the key to their success was their religion, their priests, and the abundant reminders in the form of numerous monasteries that medieval Serbia had left to them.

These factors made a significant contribution to the Serbian successes of the nineteenth century, as they worked on the resurrection of the state and the gradual emancipation from Turkish control, and the shaping of their political development. The latter involved the people's struggle to limit the powers of their monarchs and the building of democratic political institutions. In all of this, the Serbs made great if halting progress, culminating in complete success by the beginning of the twentieth century, having achieved a parliamentary democratic system.

In the early part of the twentieth century, while continuing to function as a democrat state, Serbia led in the establishment of an alliance of Balkan states that drove the Turks from Europe, and liberated some Serbian areas that had still been under Turkish control. The main action was described as the Balkan wars and the main liberated territory was Kosovo. Unfortunately for Serbia and Montenegro, the great European powers denied them some of the areas that they had liberated.

Soon thereafter, in 1914, came the First World War, which was to alter Serbia's history radically with the creation of the Kingdom of the Serbs, Croats, and Slovenes. This was the First Yugoslavia, treated in Chapter Ten above. As indicated there, that state came to an end with the German and Italian attacks in the Second World War in April 1941. During that war, the Yugoslav Communists seized power and at the end of the war created the Second Yugoslavia, i.e., Communist Yugoslavia, treated in Chapter Eleven.

As shown in that chapter, the Serbs had serious grievances with respect to their status in Communist Yugoslavia. Other republics, notably Slovenia and Croatia, also had grievances, but none of them could voice them publicly while dictator Tito was alive. As a way of preventing struggles for power after his passing, he bequeathed his successors a political system of collective leadership, with provision for due rotation among leaders of the republics in national offices held. In general, governmental bodies were modified so that virtual unanimity was required for all decisions of consequences. Tito, however, revealed his belief secretly to some persons, among them one-time governor of New York Averill Harriman and his wife, that after his death Yugoslavia would fall apart.[1]

---

[1]   Richard Cohen, *Washington Post* (January 4, 1994).

After the break with Soviet dictator Stalin, there was hope for change in dictatorial rule, and some "mellowing" did take place, but the primacy of the Communist Party was never altered. In the decade after Tito's death in 1980, his heirs sought to hold the system together, but in the end failed. In essence, the system was a failure politically, economically, and ethnically. The system bequeathed to Tito's successors led to political paralysis. The Communist Party (since 1952 called The League of Yugoslav Communists) tended to split along republic (ethnic) lines, and at an Extraordinary Congress in 1990, hopelessly divided, it breathed its last. From then, the country itself split apart.

The economy, as in other Communist-ruled countries, turned out to be a disaster. Some major economic objectives were reached, but with much waste and heavy costs. Soon after the break with Moscow, Tito did de-collectivize agriculture, but the much-touted self-management system failed to achieve expectations. Moreover, Tito's decentralizing of the economic system led to the republics engaging in ruinous competition and autarchy. In the decade after Tito's death (1980), the economy went downhill, with a huge foreign debt, high inflation, and a decline in the standard of living.

Bickering between and among the republics as to who was responsible for the sad state of economic affairs contributed to much controversy. Slovenia and Croatia claimed that they were being exploited for the benefit of the less well-to-do republics, and blamed Serbia most of all. Serbia, for its part, reminded Slovenia and Croatia, quite correctly in view of my own studies, that they had received favorable economic treatment in the First and well as in Tito's Yugoslavia, pointing out that in 1991 the average per capita income in Slovenia was $12,618, in Croatia $7,178, and in Serbia only $4,789. Moreover, Slovenia's and Croatia's profitable tourist trade was helped considerably by hams and other agricultural products from Serbia. By 1991, however, rational dialogue seemed no longer possible.

Contributing to much of the political and economic bickering was the legacy of Tito's ethnic and nationality policy. He and his Communist comrades believed that they could solve the problem of past ethnic discords by dividing the country into national republics, the first time this had been done in Yugoslavia. Some of the resulting boundaries were not rational. While Tito's handiwork may have been popular with those who wanted a separate Macedonia and Bosnia-Hercegovina, it created serious dissatisfactions, especially among the Serbs, who had been the strongest supporters of a common state and had sacrificed the most for it. Some 35 percent of them were left to live in other republics. Moreover, inside the republic of Serbia itself, two autonomous provinces were created. One was Vojvodina, where a Hungarian minority was present; the other was Kosovo, where a large Albanian majority lived.

While a part of the republic of Serbia, these provinces were subject to little or no control by Serbian authorities. This was a bitter pill, particularly the status of Kosovo, the cradle of the medieval Serbian state, where Serbia's noted religious and cultural monuments are located. Not only had Tito encouraged more and more Albanians to move into Kosovo, he also tolerated the desecration and even destruction of many of the Serbian Christian monuments by the Kosovo Albanians, who also forced thousands of Serbs to flee for fear of their lives.

During his rule, Tito managed to sweep nationality questions under the rug, insisting that those problems were solved, thereby foreclosing further dialogue on the issue. Not until Slobodan Milošević became head of the Serbian Communist party in 1986 were the Serbs able to ventilate their grievances and call for justice. The Yugoslav Communist party considered the various Serb complaints, notably in two hectic sessions of its leaders (including those from all republics) in 1987, and concluded that they had failed to find a solution to the Albanian persecution of the Serbs, but without saying so. In 1988, however, the national party amended the Yugoslav constitution, giving Serbia the right to amend its constitution, so that it could deal with its autonomous provinces. The new Serbian constitution in effect reduced the autonomy of the provinces to what it was before the 1974 Yugoslav constitution. Both Vojvodina and Kosovo gave their consent, but subsequently Kosovo attempted to take back its consent and declared that they would not accept the reduced autonomy. Then the Kosovo leaders declared that they would not participate in any government institutions—schools, police, medical clinics—and set about creating informal ones in private homes. These acts prompted Yugoslav authorities to establish a military presence in Kosovo, which the Albanians dubbed an "occupation." Shortly, the Albanians created a military insurgency.

This is getting ahead of the story of Yugoslavia's breakup, to which we shall return.

Slovenia and Croatia indicated in 1990 that they were thinking of independence when they declared their sovereignties. The Serbs, who had been the strongest supporters of a common state, nevertheless indicated that they were willing to listen to Croat and Slovene suggestions for change. When these turned out be a constitutional structure that was even weaker than the American Articles of Confederation, the Serbs made it known that they were prepared to see these republics go their own way.

Slovenia was not much of a problem since few Serbs lived there. Croatia, however, was home to 600,000 to 800,000 Serbs. The Croatian regime of General Franjo Tudjman had already reduced the Serbs to minority status, whereas in the Tito period the Serbs were on equal status with the Croats. Moreover, under Tudjman the Serbs were subjected to discriminatory acts in employment and civil rights. Cruel examples of the latter were nocturnal shootings, hate slogans painted on houses, and threatening phone calls in the middle of the night. When the Croatian authorities were unwilling to consider the complaints of the Croatian Serbs, civil conflict was not far off.

In June 1991, Slovenia and Croatia issued independence pronouncements. Slovenia took control of border posts on the Austrian and Italian borders, a clear violation of the Helsinki Accords' proviso that boundaries of internationally recognized states could not be changed except by peaceful means. The European Community (EC) intervened in the hope of finding a solution, getting Slovenia and Croatia to agree to a three-month delay.

At the end of the delay period, Slovenia and Croatia declared formal secessions, and the EC did nothing. The Yugoslav government declared the Slovene and Croat acts unconstitutional (subsequently confirmed by the Yugoslav Constitutional Court), and ordered Yugoslav Army troops in Slovenia to reclaim the border posts. The Slovenian militia, joined by irregulars, resisted fiercely, firing the first shots (downing a Yugoslav Army helicopter) in what was to evolve into a civil war. The Slovenes even seized foreign freight trucks in international transit to block highways. The result was a setback for the Yugoslav Army and its withdrawal from Slovenia.

The Slovenes and Croats insisted that the Yugoslav Constitution gave them the right to secede. While the preamble to the constitution expressed the right to self-determination, including the right to secession, the text failed to delineate actual procedures for secession. In fact, at least two articles in the Yugoslav Constitution suggested that unilateral secession was unconstitutional. Article 5 stated that the frontiers of Yugoslavia could not be altered without the consent of all the republics and autonomous provinces, and stipulated that boundaries between republics could be altered only by mutual consent. Article 240 stated that the Yugoslav armed forces were to protect the independence, sovereignty, and territorial integrity of Yugoslavia. Moreover, several articles in the federal constitution, as well as in the constitutions of the republics, outlined the responsibilities of the republics to the federation.

In subsequent efforts to blame everything on Milošević and the Serbs, Western governments and Western media declared him guilty of the fighting in Slovenia, which was not correct, because he had no position in the Yugoslav government, and was not yet even president of Serbia. Ironically, one of the witnesses against Milošević at The Hague, Slovene President Milan Kučan, was forced to admit, under Milošević's cross-examination, that Milošević was right.

Initially, as indicated above, the Western powers favored the continued existence of Yugoslavia, but Germany's hasty recognition of Slovenia and Croatia changed that. In April 1992, the United States recognized not only Slovenia and Croatia, but also Bosnia-Hercegovina. This was a clear indication that the Western Powers would respect the wishes of the Yugoslav republics that wanted to secede, but not the wishes of those republics that wanted to remain part of Yugoslavia. They did this in part by asserting that the boundaries between the republics could not be changed except by peaceful means. Ironically, as indicated above, they had already aided and abetted Slovenia and Croatia in their violation of the Helsinki Accords by using force to change the internationally recognized boundaries of Yugoslavia. At the same time, the Western Powers knew or should have known that the republic that suffered the greatest injustice when Tito carved up the country into republics and autonomous provinces was Serbia.

The fact that the Serbs were allies of the West in two world wars did not seem to matter. At the same time, their actions enabled Serbia's president, recycled Communist Slobodan Milošević, to pose as the only defender of Serbian interests, and to declare that his answer to the West would be to recognize as separate nations the Serb-inhabited areas of Croatia and Bosnia-Hercegovina.

It is important to note that at its meeting in Lisbon in February 1992, the European Community (EC) proposed a cantonal solution for Bosnia, i.e., dividing it into Serbian, Croatian, and Muslim areas. About mid-March all three Bosnian parties agreed to that solution in principle. Soon after returning to Sarajevo, however, the Muslim president, Izetbegović, reneged. The available evidence indicates that it was the United States that advised him to go back on his commitment. And the civil war in Bosnia began soon thereafter.

While it cannot be confirmed at present, there are strong reasons to believe that the president (Bush, Sr.) and his secretary of state (James Baker), determined to achieve peace in the Middle East, were being pressured by Saudi Arabia to recognize Bosnia. The Saudis, so the story goes, stressed to the United States that the Muslim leaders in Sarajevo were moderates, the type of Muslims the U.S. was relying upon in the Middle East. It is also important to note, as Secretary Baker did for some of us in July 1992, that he had been under great pressure from members of Congress who had Croatian, Slovenian, and Muslim constituents.

In any case, we need to stress that the Serbs living in Croatia and Bosnia fought against secession because of the fear of living as minorities. This fear stemmed largely from the experiences of their predecessors during World War II. The destruction of the First Yugoslavia by Germany and Italy in April 1941 was accompanied by the creation of an Axis-satellite, the Independent State of Croatia. That state, ruled by the extremist Croatian movement known as the Ustashe, controlled Croatia and most of Bosnia-Hercegovina, with approximately two million Serbs in those regions.

An influential figure in the Ustashe movement, Mile Budak, created a formula to deal with the large Serbian population: one-third to be killed; one-third forced to flee; one-third converted to Roman Catholicism. Estimates vary, but most historians on the subject agree that approximately 700,000 Serbs were brutally massacred in Croatia and Bosnia by the minions of the Ustashe regime. Some of the harshest atrocities committed against the Serbs took place in Bosnia by the Ustashe regime and the Muslims. In addition to the Serbs, other victims included approximately 60,000 Jews and 20,000 Gypsies.

The pro-Tito Croatian regime, headed by Tito's former Partisan general, Franjo Tudjman, added to Serbian fears of persecution in both Bosnia and Croatia. Prior to the outbreak of hostilities, the Croatian republic engaged in discriminatory acts in employment and civil rights against its Serbian minority. Serbs were victimized by hostile tactics, including vandalism. In addition, the Tudjman regime adopted some of the symbols and trappings of the hated Ustashe state. Furthermore, while Croatia's pre-independence constitution viewed the Croats and Serbs as equals, the new text created after the secession reduced the Serbs to minority status.

In Bosnia, the "Islamic Declaration," authored by Muslim leader Alija Izetbegović, issued in 1970 and re-issued in 1990, also gave the Bosnian Serbs, as well as Bosnian Croats, reason for alarm. The Declaration stated that the Islamic movement should seize power once it is "morally and numerically strong enough," and that "there can be neither peace nor co-existence between the Islamic religion and non-Islamic social and political institutions." The Declaration further stated:

> [the] upbringing of the people, and particularly means of mass influence—the press, radio, television, and film—should be in the hands of people whose Islamic moral and intellectual authority is indisputable. The media should not be allowed—as so often happens—to fall into the hands of perverted and degenerate people who then transmit the aimlessness and emptiness of their lives to others.

These pronouncements were in sharp contrast to the Muslim assertions during the civil war, i.e., that they wished to live in peace and harmony with Serbs, Croats, Jews, and other Bosnians.

Western Response to Yugoslavia's Breakup

After the 1991 secessions and ensuing hostilities, the EC's initial response was to organize a mission to Yugoslavia, led by former British Foreign Secretary, Lord Carrington. The hope was for a peaceful settlement. This was the time when U.S. Secretary of State, James Baker, had declared that if Yugoslavia were to break up, Washington would wait until the various factions had resolved their differences through political settlements before deciding on the question of diplomatic recognition. Simultaneously, Baker personally warned the Slovenian and Croatian leaders that unilateral secessions would result in civil war.

Former U.S. Secretary of State, Cyrus Vance, who had replaced Lord Carrington and United Nations Secretary General, Javier Perez de Cuellar, both warned the Western Powers that premature recognition of Slovenia and Croatia could intensify and widen the war. But Western policy-makers seemingly did not weigh the consequences of their acts or did not care. The Western response to the Yugoslav conflict was summarized by a political science professor at an academic gathering in November 1992 as follows: "The West came to Yugoslavia as fire fighters and ended up as pyromaniacs."

For some strange reason, the West proceeded on the assumption that the Serbs ought to forget their enormous past sacrifices and abuses, and simply be satisfied to have three million of their compatriots revert once again to foreign rule. The Serbs pointed out that their objective was not the creation of some mystical empire, but only to safeguard the rights of Serbs who had lived in a common state since 1918.

Instead of examining their policies, the Western leaders and the Western media insisted on blaming almost all of the deaths and destruction on the Serbs and Serbia. They continued to talk of a "Serbian-dominated Yugoslavia," ignoring the fact that prior to the secessions, key positions in the Yugoslav government were held by non-Serbs. The prime minister, Ante Marković and Foreign Minister Budimir Lončar were Croats. The minister of defense and supreme commander of the armed forces, General Kadijević, was the son of a Serbian-Croatian marriage. The deputy commander of the armed forces, Stane Brovet, was a Slovene. And the chief of the air force, Zvonko Jurjević, was another Croat.

In the meantime, Vance and his group came up with a plan to settle the Bosnian situation, but the Clinton administration vetoed it. None of the Bosnian parties were enthusiastic, but Vance and his collaborators believed that they could have been forced to go along if it had not been for the Clinton veto. And the Europeans were still determined. Vance was replaced by Lord David Owen, former British foreign secretary. Owen labored relentlessly, with Thorvald Stoltenberg, one-time Norwegian ambassador to Belgrade, as Co-Chairman. They produced several peace plans, but the Clinton administration vetoed them as before. Differing justifications were put forth, but the major one was that the plans were unfair to the Muslims.

Finally, the Clinton administration decided to force a settlement by bombing the Bosnian Serbs into submission. In the intervening months there were three explosions at Sarajevo markets for which Serbs were blamed. No proof was ever offered of Serb culpability, and independent investigators concluded that the Serbs were not guilty, and that the most likely guilty parties were Muslims or their friends.

Also, in those months the Serbs were condemned for shelling several Bosnian cities that the Security Council had declared to be "safe havens." The Clinton administration paid little attention to warnings by the United Nations Secretary General, Boutros Boutros-Ghali, that the United States and its allies were guilty of violating international conventions that provided that such supposedly safe havens had to be demilitarized. The Clinton crowd did not seem to be bothered by the Muslims using those "safe havens" to launch attacks against the Serbs. Lord Owen categorized the Security Council proclamation of the safe-areas as "the most irresponsible decision taken during my time as Co-Chairman."[2]

But the U.S. was determined, and eventually forced a settlement at a U.S.-sponsored meeting in November 1995 at the U.S. Air Force facility at Dayton, Ohio. The new Bosnian state is made up of two parts, the Muslim-Croat federation and the Bosnian Serb Republic. The central authority is extremely weak, and much decision-making is done by the West's High Representative in Sarajevo, who was authorized to make

---

2 *Balkan Odyssey* (New York: Harcourt Brace, 1995), p. 178.

decisions if the central authority failed to do so. He made decisions concerning auto licenses, the nation's flag, the currency, etc. He also has the authority to nullify decisions of the Muslim-Croat unit and the Serb Republic, and has done so. He even nullified the election of the president of the Serb Republic because he believed that the president-elect did not really accept the Dayton decisions.

In 2003, the High Representative, Lord Ashdown, violated the Dayton Peace Accord by merging the Republika Srpska intelligence service into the Islamist-controlled—and bin Laden linked—intelligence service of the Federation. Instead of safeguarding Dayton, Ashdown has violated it.

As of this writing (2003), seven years have passed since Dayton, and there is no conviction among experts that the Bosnian state will survive.

For the Serbs, worse days were still to come. There was and still is Kosovo. Once in power, as indicated above, Communist dictator Tito divided Yugoslavia into six republics and two autonomous provinces, both of the latter in Serbia: Vojvodina, with a large Hungarian minority, and Kosovo, with an Albanian majority. The autonomous powers of Kosovo were steadily increased, reaching its maximum in the Yugoslav Constitution of 1974. Under the latter, Kosovo was in all but name a republic. It could even veto bills in the Serbian parliament that had nothing to do with Kosovo, whereas Serbia had no comparable power with respect to Kosovo. Government in Kosovo was in the hands of the Kosovo Communist Party, part and parcel of the national party. The large majority of the Kosovo party were Albanians, with a minority of Serb Communists.

From the beginning, the Kosovo Albanians were determined to make Kosovo ethnically Albanian. Among other things, they brought in professors and textbooks from Albania, and they encouraged migrations of Albanians from Albania to Kosovo.

The Kosovo Serbs had grievances, but these never reached Belgrade until 1969, when a Serbian Orthodox petition reached Tito, who expressed disbelief but promised to look into the matter. Nothing happened. After Tito's death in 1980, evidence of discriminatory acts against Kosovo Serbs increased. Among those acts were: Albanian seizure and/or destruction of Serbian properties (burning of haystacks and buildings, cutting down fruit trees, Serbs selling properties to Albanians under duress, etc.), damage and/or destruction and desecration of church properties and cemeteries.

For several years, the Serbian Bar Association worked assiduously to get action from national institutions, with meager results aside from promises. The cleansing of Serbs from Kosovo is best illustrated by some statistics. In 1961, for example, the percentage of Serbs in Kosovo was 27.4, while the Albanians were 67.1. In 1991, the percentage of Serbs dropped to 11.0, while the Albanians had gone up to 81.6.

In the meantime, the Communist Party of Yugoslavia (formally League) was constantly confronted by the discriminatory acts against the Kosovo Serbs. In May and June 1987, the leaders from all the republics and autonomous provinces held two hectic conferences in efforts to deal with the persecution of Kosovo Serbs, but concluded that they could not find a solution.

In 1988, the national party amended the Yugoslav Constitution, giving Serbia the right to amend its constitution so as to deal with the autonomous provinces. The new Serbian constitution (1989) took away the right of the provinces to veto acts of the Serbian parliament. This constitution was ratified by Vojvodina and Kosovo, although the latter subsequently sought to revoke its act.

The new Serbian constitution did not revoke Kosovo's autonomy, but reduced it to what it was under the 1963 Yugoslav Constitution. The Kosovo Albanians rejected the decrease and engaged in civil disobedience. They refused to participate in all government institutions—schools, police, medical facilities—and set about creating their informal ones in homes and elsewhere. And they went on strikes in government enterprises, which resulted in firings.

The government in Belgrade, at that time headed by Slobodan Milošević, established a military presences in the province, which the Albanians dubbed an "occupation."

In the mid- and late 1990s, the Kosovo Albanians began killing Kosovo officials (Serbs, Albanians and others). In short, the Belgrade government had a full-scale insurgency on its hands. It proceeded to deal with it the way any government would, with force.

United States and NATO Intervention

The United States sought to promote a peaceful settlement. U.S. negotiator Richard C. Holbrooke worked out an agreement with Milošević that provided: (1) Serbian and Yugoslav forces that were moved to Kosovo during 1998 be withdrawn and a cease-fire be established; (2) negotiations for a political settlement should proceed, and (3) NATO verifiers be introduced in Kosovo.

It was soon evident that this agreement held little hope for a settlement. As soon as the Serb-Yugoslav forces were withdrawn, instead of a cease-fire, the Kosovo Liberation Army (KLA) moved into the areas that the Serbs had controlled and proceeded to kill Serb officials as well as civilians. The KLA strategy was to get the Serbs to over-react, thereby bringing the U.S. to their side.

In January 1999, some 40-odd Albanian men were killed at the area of Raćek. The U.S. immediately blamed the Serbs, even though there was no conclusive evidence. The Albanians had dug a trench all around the town. One Serb military officer was quoted as saying that Serb guards had killed the men guarding the trenches, and then there was a gun battle. The Serbs had actually invited observers for the next day, when they would tackle Raćek. International press reports from Raćek did not blame the Serbs for the alleged massacre.

The U.S. called a conference in the hope of promoting a settlement. Its proposal favored the Albanians, among other things giving them the right to vote for independence after three years. This was the proposal that the U.S. presented at Rambouillet, France, in February 1999. It seemed acceptable to all the major powers, including Russia. There were hints that the Serbs would agree. Then U.S. Secretary of State Albright introduced a special annex that would give NATO the right not only to occupy Kosovo, but that NATO would also have unrestricted access to all of Yugoslavia. Milošević was told either to accept or NATO would bomb. Yugoslavia refused, and in March 1999 NATO began bombing the Serbs for what turned out to be 78 days. Canada's onetime ambassador to Yugoslavia, James Bissett, has called attention to the fact that Britain's Defense Minister, Lord Gilbert, in July 2000 told the British House of Commons that the terms forced upon Serbia's president,

Slobodan Milošević, at Rambouillet were deliberately designed to provoke the war.[3]

The Serbs charged that the bombing was the epitome of the arrogance of the Clinton administration, characterized especially by his Secretary of State, Madeleine Albright. There was no seeking of authorization from the United Nations. The bombing was even a violation of the NATO treaty, which asserted in part: "The parties undertake, as set forth in the Charter of the United Nations, to settle any international dispute in which they may be involved, by peaceful means in such a manner that international peace and security and justice are not endangered...."

Yugoslavia did not violate the border of any NATO country. It did not violate the border of any member of the United Nations. It did not threaten any state enjoying international recognition.

In April 1999, thirty-one members of the U.S. Congress filed a bipartisan lawsuit to require the president to obtain either a declaration of war or specify statutory authorization from Congress in order to continue the war in Yugoslavia. A federal judge dismissed the suit on technical grounds.

President Clinton had asserted that the aim of the NATO attack was to bring about a democratic, multi-ethnic Kosovo. Four years after the Serb forces withdrew, there is not even a hint that such an achievement is remotely possible.

The Serbs withdrew under conditions spelled out by United Nations document Number 1244, part of which asserts that Kosovo remains an integral part of Yugoslavia. Its other provisions about various progress steps toward a democratic, multi-ethnic Kosovo remain unfulfilled. Despite the UN and NATO forces in Kosovo, the Albanians have achieved the opposite. Over 200,000 Kosovo Serbs have been expelled. Many have been killed. Some have been kidnapped and there is no accounting concerning their whereabouts. Other Kosovo minorities have received similar treatment. Serbian churches and monasteries have been destroyed and/or damaged. The Serbs that remain are living in enclaves under close protection of NATO or UN authorities. Some Serbs would like to return, but that is highly unlikely.

---

[3] *Byronica* (Chicago), July 2003, p. 3.

The Kosovo Albanians assert freely that they have no desire for a multi-ethnic Kosovo. They and their friends abroad are campaigning for an independent Kosovo. And no one seems ready for a partition that would give the Serbs a minimum "bone."

For several years before the NATO war, a number of Balkan experts suggested a partitioning of Kosovo. Unfortunately, the Clinton administration ignored all such ideas, and that at a time when the United States could have forced the acceptance of such a solution. And there would have been no reason for war. It seems that Clinton-Albright listened only to the Albanians.

The U.S. led the NATO attack on a sovereign country that had not been accused of any violation of the United Nations Charter or the NATO treaty, or even that Yugoslavia had threatened any such violations, is a most serious undermining of the nation-state system. The notion that a state is sovereign when it involves its domestic affairs dates back to the Peace of Westphalia of 1648. Other developments over the centuries have tended to strengthen that doctrine. The fact that Yugoslavia was a charter member of the League of Nations and of the United Nations merely adds to the seriousness of the United States action.

The U.S.-NATO action was defended on the grounds that it was necessary to come to the rescue of a minority, the Kosovo Albanians, but subsequent investigations question even the accuracy of that contention. Practically all of the alleged atrocities proved unfounded. What concerned many international law authorities was the precedent that was set. Presumably, any nation or combination of nations could now find that some minority needs rescue, and could proceed to act, justifying such action on the U.S.-NATO precedent. In any case, the nation-state system may be an "endangered species."

* * *

As the strongest supporters of a Yugoslav state, the Serbs lived to see those dreams shattered at great cost and with incredible sacrifices. Communism was the ultimate of downhill movements for the Serbs, even greater, in the opinion of many Serbs, than the defeat at Kosovo by the Ottoman Turks. The end of the Second Yugoslavia came in the year 2000 with the overthrow of the Milošević regime. A new era began, with countless problems facing the Serbs. In 2003, the Yugoslav state, including Montenegro, got a new name—Serbia-Montenegro. New generations of Serbs now face the task of building the future of their new nation.

Selected Bibliography

Armstrong, Hamilton Fish. *Tito and Goliath.* New York: Macmillan, 1951.

Beloff, Nora. *Tito's Flawed Legacy: Yugoslavia and the West Since 1939.* Boulder, CO: East European Monographs, 1985.

Burg, Steven L. and Paul Shoup. *The War in Bosnia-Herzegovina: Ethnic Conflict and International Intervention.* Armonk, NY: M. E. Sharpe, 1999.

Corwin, Phillip. *Dubious Mandate: A Memoir of the UN in Bosnia, September 1995.* Durham, NC: Duke University Press, 1999.

Dempsey, Gary T. (ed.). *Exiting the Balkan Thicket.* Washington, DC: Cato Institute, 2002.

Djilas, Aleksa. *The Contested Country: Yugoslav Unity and Communist Revolution, 1919–1953.* Cambridge, MA: Harvard University Press, 1991.

Djilas, Milovan. *The New Class: An Analysis of the Communist System.* New York: Praeger, 1957.

Djordjevic, Dimitrije. *The Creation of Yugoslavia, 1914–1918.* Santa Barbara, CA: Clio Books, 1983.

Dragnich, Alex N. *The Development of Parliamentary Government in Serbia.* Boulder, CO: East European Monographs, 1978.

_____. *The Destruction of Yugoslavia and the Struggle for Truth.* Boulder, CO: East European Monographs, 1995.

_____. *The First Yugoslavia: Search for a Viable Political System.* Stanford, CA: Hoover Institution Press, 1983.

_____. *Serbia, Nikola Pašić, and Yugoslavia.* New Brunswick, NJ: Rutgers University Press, 1974.

_____. *Serbs and Croats: The Struggle in Yugoslavia.* New York: Harcourt Brace, 1992.

_____. *Tito's Promised Land: Yugoslavia.* New Brunswick, NJ: Rutgers University Press, 1954.

Dragnich, Alex N. and Slavko Todorovich. *The Saga of Kosovo: Focus on Serbian-Albanian Relations.* Boulder, CO: East European Monographs, 1984.

Fleming, Thomas. *Montenegro: The Divided Land.* Rockford, IL: Chronicles Press, 2003.

Glenny, Misha. *The Fall of Yugoslavia: The Third Balkan War.* New York: Penguin, 1996.

Holbrooke, Richard. *To End a War.* New York: Random House, 1998.

Hoptner, Jacob. *Yugoslavia in Crisis, 1934–1941.* New York: Columbia University Press, 1962.

Hudson, Kate. *Breaking the South Slav Dream: The Rise and Fall of Yugoslavia.* London: Pluto Press, 2003.

Job, Cvijeto. *Yugoslavia's Ruin: The Bloody Lessons of Nationalism. A Patriot's Warning.* Lanham, MD: Rowan & Littlefield, 2002.

Johnstone, Diana. *Fool's Crusade: Yugoslavia, NATO, and Western Delusions.* New York: Monthly Review Press, 2002.

Judah, Tim. *The Serbs: History, Myth, and the Destruction of Yugoslavia.* New Haven, CT: Yale University Press, 1997.

Jukic, Ilija. *The Fall of Yugoslavia.* New York: Harcourt Brace Jovanovich, 1974.

Lees, Michael. *The Rape of Serbia: The British Role in Tito's Grab for Power, 1943–1944.* New York: Harcourt Brace Jovanovich, 1990.

Martin, David. *The Web of Disinformation: Churchill's Yugoslav Blunder.* New York: Harcourt Brace Jovanovich, 1990.

Owen, David. *Balkan Odyssey.* New York: Harcourt Brace, 1995.

Parenti, Michael. *To Kill a Nation: The Attack on Yugoslavia.* London: Verso, 2000.

Pavlovich, Paul. *The Serbians: The Story of a People.* Toronto, 1983.

Pavlowitch, Steven K. *The Improbable Survivor.* London: C. Hurst, 1988.

Petrovich, Michael B. *History of Modern Serbia,* 2 vols. New York: Harcourt Brace Jovanovich, 1976.

Ranke, Leopold von. *The History of Serbia and the Serbian Revolution.* New York: 1973.

Roberts, Walter R. *Tito, Mihailovich, and the Allies, 1941–1945.* New Brunswick, NJ: Rutgers University Press, 1973.

Rusinow, Dennison. *The Yugoslav Experiment: 1948–1974.* Berkeley, CA: University of California Press, 1977.

Sirc, Ljubo. *The Yugoslav Economy Under Self-Management.* London: Macmillan, 1979.

Temperely, Harold W. *History of Serbia.* London, 1917.

Vucinich, Wayne (ed.). *The First Serbian Uprising, 1804–1813.* Boulder, CO: East European Monographs, 1982.

_____. *Serbia Between East and West: The Events of 1903–1908.* Stanford, CA: Stanford University Press, 1954.

West, Rebecca. *Black Lamb and Grey Falcon: A Journey Through Yugoslavia.* New York: Penguin, 1982.

Woodward, Susan L. *Balkan Tragedy: Chaos and Dissolution After the Cold War.* Washington, DC: Brookings Institution, 1995.